D0866932

LORE FERGUSON WILBERT

HANDLE

WITH CARE

HOW JESUS REDEEMS THE POWER
OF TOUCH IN LIFE AND MINISTRY

PUBLISHING
NASHVILLE, TENNESSEE

978-1-5359-6233-9

Published by B&H Publishing Group
Nashville, Tennessee

Dewey Decimal Classification: 152.1
Subject Heading: TOUCH / HUGGING / SENSES AND
SENSATION

Unless otherwise noted, all Scripture quotations are taken
from the Christian Standard Bible®, copyright © 2017 by
Holman Bible Publishers. Used by permission. Christian
Standard Bible® and CSB® are federally registered trademarks
of Holman Bible Publishers.

Also used: English Standard Version (esv), ESV® Text
Edition: 2016. Copyright © 2001 by Crossway Bibles, a
publishing ministry of Good News Publishers.

Also used: New Living Translation (nlt), copyright © 1996,
2004, 2015 by Tyndale House Foundation. Used by
permission of Tyndale House Publishers, Inc.,
Carol Stream, Illinois 60188. All rights reserved.

Also used: The Message (msg), Copyright © 1993,
2002, 2018 by Eugene H. Peterson.

Published in association with the literary agency of
William K. Jensen Literary Agency, 119 Bampton Court,
Eugene, Oregon 97404

Cover design and illustration by Stephen Crotts.
Author photo by Janine Bergey.

1 2 3 4 5 6 7 8 • 24 23 22 21 20

To Nathan Andrew, whose hands bless and never curse,
heal and never harm, serve and never withhold.

Acknowledgments

I was never one who just knew she would write a book someday. I never burned inside with desire to see my name on a cover. In some ways, it embarrasses me that this book has been written and my name is, indeed, on the cover. This book should have the names of all those who gently (and sometimes not so gently) prodded me along the way for the past twenty-two years, since I first exercised my writing muscles.

To Mykl, for never letting me get away with lazy writing, even at fifteen years old.

To Nan, for making me write and rewrite, for being "believey" in me when I certainly didn't believe in myself.

To Tony, for giving me affirmation that kept me writing for years.

To my agent, Bill, for sticking with me all these years, with all these fits and starts, proposals and plummets, and hemming and hawing.

To Matt, for all the ways you have shepherded and loved me. I love Jesus at my core because of your relentless determination to speak His name above all others.

To Grant, Soley, and Lindsey for the title.

To my first readers, Mason, Haley, Greg, J'Layne, Kelly, Steve, Rachel, and KJ, your pushback and encouragement was right and good and needed.

To Kelsey, who went above and beyond on the first edit of this book and made all the disparate pieces fit.

To Chandler, for organizing my life and work cheerfully. (Write everyday; don't stop.)

To Jennifer, for telling me all those years ago that if I ever wrote a book, you wanted to publish it.

To Ashley, for being an excellent and thorough editor. And to the whole B&H Team for taking a wild chance on a first-time author with a weird book idea.

To my Sayable.net readers. You have cheered me, corrected me, spurred me on to love and good works, notified me of typos, supported me with your messages and encouragement for almost twenty years. *Sayable* exists because of you, and therefore I write because of you.

To my church family, to whom it's no secret I don't run at a high capacity. Thank you for the grace and time I needed to do the work this subject needed and never putting pressure on me to serve at a higher capacity than I was able. Thank you, specifically to my Home Group for being excited every step of the way and for being generous huggers.

To Janine, to whom the idea of personal space is unheard of. I am better for it. I am most at home when I am near you. This book was birthed in our friendship and formed by it more than I can ever express with words.

And to Nathan, for being my best confidant, encourager, challenger, and toucher. I think this book was waiting for you and I could not have written it without the honor of being your wife and having you in my life. Your hands were one of the first things I noticed about you, sitting across from me in Connection Central, turning the pages of your Bible, scribing notes in the margins. Of all the things I love about you, it is the way you use your hands—to love, to cherish, to serve, to rest, to shepherd, and to care—I love you most.

To God, who formed, knit, and crafted every human body that has ever existed and imprinted them each with Your own image. What a generous Creator You are.

Contents

Introduction

T he house was built in the late 1700s, crumbling plaster and creaking floorboards its proof. In the back room is a small woodstove, and it is here I have one of my first memories. It is my neighbor's home.

I am two years old, and it is a frigid day outside and nearly as cold inside in this uninsulated back room. An older child (My brother? My babysitter? A neighbor?) pulls off my winter boots, takes off my striped snow encrusted mittens, and shimmies me out of my red snowsuit, as I stand there shivering, waiting for what's next.

I feel the warmth of the woodstove to my back and I begin to lean into it, whipped suddenly forward by this older child's hands. "Don't touch that!" they yell at me.

My face crumbles into shock and fear. I don't know what I've done wrong, but I feel the wrath in their warning. "It's hot! It will burn you." I am still young enough that I don't even know what "burned" is. I turn and face the warmth again until I am yanked back again, and my chapped and cold hands are slapped for disobedience.

My first memory in this world is being told to not touch something without knowing why, and many of my memories since have been confusing because of the same warning: *Do not touch*. It is not lost on me that I was slapped to keep from being burnt, hurt to keep from being hurt. From my first memory, I have been confused about touch.

I am not alone.

In the Old Testament books of law, there is a form of one statement made thirty-eight times: "Do not touch." There are rules about razors that should never touch heads and laws about hands that shouldn't touch parts of the tabernacle. Laws about not touching the sick, bleeding, feeble, and diseased. Mandates about not touching work on the Sabbath and not touching the belongings of wicked people. Rules about not touching particular animals, not touching women during their menstruation cycles or after they give birth, and not touching a man's semen. Laws about not touching holy things and unholy things. Not touching holy men and unholy men.

Touching so many things was forbidden to most of God's people. Only the high priests were allowed to handle what was considered holy, and only after extensive cleansing rituals before and after.

But a curious thing happens in the New Testament when Jesus begins His ministry:

He touches.

Jesus touches the feeble and the women, the bleeding and the unclean, and the heads of adulterous women. He heals on the Sabbath using His hands. He touches the diseased and the children. He allows Himself to be touched too, by unclean people, women, snot-nosed kids, tax collectors, and sinners. On the last day before Jesus' crucifixion, we even see Him reclining with John, who leaned back against Him to ask a question. Jesus came to fulfill the law and to make what was unclean, clean. And one of the ways He did this was through touching. Even a woman suffering from bleeding twelve years merely *touched* His robe and she was made clean and—this is important—He knew He had been touched because He felt the power go out of Him. He felt the *cost* of the touch.

To touch is to be vulnerable and to be touched is to be vulnerable too. I think of a friend of mine who adopted a newborn and sat in a Neonatal Intensive Care Unit for days, her shirt undone, the babe pressed against her bare chest. The baby not of her flesh becoming part of her flesh, exposed, but for the sake of another. For the sake of his health, his maturation, and his attachment, she became vulnerable for him.

This is what Jesus did in the New Testament. He became the most vulnerable by having His body touched most wickedly, ten-inch nails driven into His flesh, thorns digging into His scalp, stripped naked, a spear thrust into His side. He gave His body to be broken, to be handled in weakness for the sake of righteousness. The crucifixion was the cruelest and most life-destroying form of touch a person could ever experience.

The resurrection was a different story. Three days later when He rose again, one of the first acts of the risen Lord is an invitation to life-giving touch. The weak-faithed Thomas said, "If I don't see the mark of the nails in his hands, put my finger into the mark of the nails, and put my hand into his side, I will never believe."[1] So Jesus invited him to do what? *Touch.* Place his fingers in the marks of the nails, put his hands on the spear-pierced side.

In the presence of weak faith—a wholly intangible thing—Jesus says a most tangible thing: Touch and be touched.

Most humans are born with all five senses—taste, touch, hearing, smell, and sight—but of the five, touch is one of the three fully developed at birth.[2] At birth, it is touch we need most and most instantly. Sight, smell, taste, hearing, these can and do wait—developing over the next few years. But touch, and the lack of it, is felt immediately. I believe God created us this way on purpose.

We're in a time in history when on one hand, reports of inappropriate or sinful touch are commonplace, and abuse is tragically alive and well, even in the church. In these cases, touch has been forced, and it causes all sorts of damage. On the other hand, we are also living in a time when even a mere glance can be interpreted as sexual harassment. For fear of being touched the wrong way, any indication of warmth or interest or even friendship is warded off and labeled as wrong.

Parents are anxious about touching even their own children for fear of repercussions years away. Or sometimes children shirk from their parents' touch or parents withhold it

---

[1] John 20:25.
[2] https://infantino.com/blogs/the-baby-monitor/sensory-development -your-baby-s-first-year-milestones-infographic.

simply because it's uncomfortable, or they're not sure how to express it healthily. Rule upon rule exist in nurseries, schools, and youth groups to prevent even the hint of anything inappropriate—and still, reports of abuse are common.

As for opposite genders, especially in the church, quick side hugs or no hugging at all is the norm. Marriage is happening later and later for many, and those in prolonged seasons of singleness have no outlet for healthy human touch. And if a marriage does take place, all touch is interpreted as sexual or foreplay, and because of this paradigm, it is withheld or taken wrongfully.

We go through life tense with anxiety, unhappy with life, and afraid of so much. Because we are critical of touch we don't understand, we end up dealing with these things by paying for touch from strangers in the form of massage or pedicures, when most of us probably just need a hug from someone who actually knows and cares for us.

Hugs alone—or intentional firm touch, like massage— have been proven to lower stress, lower heart rates in adults, regulate body temperature in infants, and lessen fears. Merely ten or twenty seconds of firm contact between adults, adults and children, children and children, and even humans and animals, can accomplish all of the above. A hug!

Yet, as the squeamish looks I get when I mention this book project indicate, most of our thoughts immediately run in the direction of erotic touch when we talk about touch at all. It's as if we cannot separate good, healthy, normal human touch from what we envision to be its most intimate case scenario—or its most perverted forms. Sexual touch is not a worst-case scenario, but since sexual touch is meant to be reserved for one man and one woman within the confines of marriage, it has a limitation on it in time, space, and person, and limitations scare us.

Since the garden of Eden, we have pressed back against limitations and added to what God has said. In Genesis 2, God did not say Adam and Eve could not *touch* the tree of knowledge, only that they could not *eat* from it. But Eve added to what God said when she answered the enemy's question, "Did God *really* say, 'You can't eat from any tree in the garden'?" "God said, 'You must not eat it *or* touch it, or you will die,'"[3] Eve responded. We've been doing the same ever since.

Most of us are legalists from birth and to protect ourselves, we draw the lines farther and farther from the truth. Sexual touch is meant solely for marriage, but God did not say we cannot touch our fathers and mothers, brothers and sisters, children and friends, uncles and aunts, pastors and congregations, old folks and young ones, singles and marrieds, and the list goes on. For fear of sinful sexual touch (erotic touch outside the covenant of marriage), we limit all or most touch.

Yet our bodies are very literally *aching* to be touched.

John Piper shared a story years ago about a woman who would cut herself intentionally on her abdomen and need to be taken to the emergency room. This happened several times and once when he was in there to visit her, he had a conversation with her. His experience went like this:

---

[3] Genesis 3:1–3, emphasis added.

"Can you give me any light or help on what goes on in your head? Why are you doing this?" And what I remember she said was, "I like it when they touch me in the emergency room."

So here's one analysis of one person—namely, me. And I don't want to generalize this. Here is a woman who . . . probably felt very alone, very untouched, very unloved, very un-cared for. She watched the whole world going its way with people hugging each other and loving each other and having friends or being married. And she had this unbelievable ache in her heart to be cared for, to be pitied, to be touched and ministered to. And her unhealthy way of doing it was to hurt herself.[4]

Piper goes on to mention that there are probably people out there who haven't been hugged in a decade or more—one of which he even spoke with in his church. He finishes by saying:

It was just so revelatory for me for a moment that there are people who actually go through life [like this]—and they are good people! They're not eager to jump into bed as a

---

[4] John Piper, "How Would You Offer Hope to Someone Who Is Addicted to Cutting Himself?" *Desiring God*, February 9, 2010, https://www.desiringgod.org/interviews/how-would-you-offer-hope-to-someone-who-is-addicted-to-cutting-himself.

prostitute or to fool around on the weekend. They know they're going to be pure—but they're not ever touched. Nobody ever touches them. And so I thought, "Boy. God, make me a good hugger. Make me a good, clean, pure, trusted, pastoral hugger." And I'm probably not the best at it. Some people are like hugging trees, and others like hugging big panda bears. And others like hugging bean bags. Some people are just really good at hugging. And I just want to be one of those.[5]

What does it mean to be a "good, clean, pure, trusted, pastoral hugger"? In an age when touch between two people, adults or children, is almost always taken or received as its most inappropriate form, what does it mean to be good at touch? Clean in our touch? Pure touchers? Trusted touchers? And pastoral in our touching?

※ ※ ※

In this book, I will walk us through eight scenarios in which we will need to practice touch throughout life. I say practice because this requires learning what isn't natural, much in the same way we practice musical scales or practice a sport. Our practice of touch in culture and the church is woefully underdeveloped and I want to help us think critically and biblically about the example Christ set for us.

---

[5] Ibid.

I will say this again and again in this book: my aim will not be to give you how-tos or examples of healthy touch. This is not the purpose of *Handle with Care*. My emphasis is always going to be on how we *care* more than on how we *handle*. I am concerned first about the hearts of the reader before the hands of the reader. If you're combing through this book looking for prescriptive advice about how to specifically touch children, spouses, friends, or neighbors, what's permissible and what's not, you won't find it. This is on purpose.

Because I am this book's author, I will also weave my personal thoughts, ideas, and story throughout each chapter, including a chapter sharing my experience of touch throughout life. I cannot help but be informed by my own story; and while my story may not be common, ordinary, or the rule, I cannot divorce it from my perspective and still bring empathy to this book. "The danger of this approach," as Zack Eswine says in *Sensing Jesus*, "as with any of us who seek to testify about God in our own and others' lives, is to leave the reader with more of a sense of us than of Jesus. On the other hand, the danger of eschewing a more personal approach is to try to point us to Jesus as if he has nothing to do with the real sights, sounds, and providence of his creation under the sun."[6] My narrative within is not meant to be prescriptive, but merely descriptive of the experiences God has used to inform my view of Him and the interactions with people Jesus had in Scripture. We are embodied people, and as Jen Pollock Michel would say, "the lessons we often best absorb

---

[6] Zack Eswine, *Sensing Jesus* (Wheaton, IL: Crossway, 2013), 25.

are the ones we learn with our senses."[7] This is true for all of us, regardless of how disassociated from our bodies we feel at times. I hope my story will not only lend empathy to how I speak about touch, but will also create empathy in you as you read *Handle with Care*. Even more, I hope reading this book creates empathy in you as you interact with your own body and the bodies around you.

What could it mean for the family, singles, marriages, the church, the community, and the world to have good, healthy, pure, faithful, ministering touch? Where is our faith weak concerning this? Perhaps our faith is weak in this area because we have not been touched enough. Perhaps it is because we have been touched sinfully and we cannot find freedom from this act against us. Or maybe because we have touched sinfully and our conscience condemns us. Or perhaps because we're squeamish about germs or strangers or snotty-nosed kids or women with breasts or men who won't let go. I don't know. I can't know. But I do know that somewhere in the mess of our beliefs, assumptions, and fears about touch, there is something whole and beautiful and good and God-given in there. As Jesus shows us with His own life, there is ministry in touching.

---

[7] Jen Pollock Michel, *Teach Us to Want* (Downers Grove, IL: InterVarsity Press Books 2014), 136.

CHAPTER ONE

Using Our Hands to Live

Touch has a memory.[1]
—John Keats

W e used our hands in our home—to speak, punish, work, play, and love. And it was not an undemonstrative home. It was a rowdy, creative, busy household, and I was the only girl of eight children.

Thirty years ago the ten acres on which we lived in Bucks County, Pennsylvania, was grown thick with trees and covered with boulders, brush, and bloodroot. It was the perfect place to raise a brood of boys and their tomboy sister. At night we lay tangled in crocheted blankets around the living room listening to my mother read aloud, and those stories came alive

---

[1] John Keats, "What Can I Do to Drive Away," *Complete Poems and Selected Letters of John Keats* (New York: Modern Library, a division of Random House, 2001), 361.

during our day. We were cops and robbers, orphans and bandits, pirates and sailors. The last words we heard when heading out to play were: "Don't come back until dark unless you're bleeding." We knew that quite literally to mean we were not to come back unless we were quite literally bleeding—which was an often-enough occurrence that the emergency room at our local hospital knew the Fergusons by name. I don't think any of us has broken a bone or needed stitches fewer than eight times each.

We were a tactile bunch then and now, as adults scattered throughout the United States with our respective spouses, significant others, and children. When we get together at my mom and her husband's house, I am not there more than ten minutes before I have an adult brother rubbing my shoulders, poking me in the side, or dropping a languid arm around my shoulders.

I may be the second oldest, but I am without question the shortest, a fact about which my youngest brother—twenty years my junior—finds every opportunity to mention. He was fewer than two pounds when he was born nearly three months premature; I could once cup my hand in a C shape and tent it over his entire torso, my fingertips touching on either side of his NICU incubator mattress without my palm and the fragile skin of his chest touching one another. I'm delighted his now fully-grown man arms can rest atop my head when I visit.

Even though we were happy as a rowdy and tactile family, there was sometimes an aggressive atmosphere in our male-dominated home that didn't fit my disposition. At a young age I was aware that the way I touched and wanted to be touched was somehow different and foreign from the way our household treated it. I didn't like to wrestle. I didn't even like it when my brothers wrestled. I didn't like to be shoved and shuffled. But I also didn't like to be kissed on my cheek or neck as my dad was prone to doing. I was deeply uncomfortable with the assumption that everyone ought to welcome touch in the manner in which it was initiated. I believed if someone wanted to tickle me (which I despised then and now), I had to accept that my bigger and stronger brothers would pin my arms down and I would be tickled. The same went for wrestling: if one wanted to engage in it, the assumption was the other *had* to engage in it. The same for kisses on my neck from my dad or a hug from one of my brothers. If I said no or expressed I was uncomfortable, I was made to feel guilty for not being tougher or not being the kind of little girl who *liked* her daddy's kisses. Permission to say "no" wasn't given, wasn't even an option. Touch was non-negotiable. And that made it something I endured more than I appreciated.

Touch wasn't always this fraught for me, though. As a small child, I remember loving it when my mother would rub small circles on my back or scratch my arm while I was draped across her lap. This strong woman birthed eight babies and the option of not being touched for one single second of the day might have been a welcome one, but she never refused our request for a back-scratch or a hug. I still think of her enveloping hugs when I hug someone today. They were warm and ample and tight, the way a hug ought to be.

This is not a memoir or a tell-all, so, reader, you'll have to forgive my vague allusion to certain details of the story, but at a young age I was sexually abused. This is when, if I trace my memories back correctly, my aversion to being touched without asking for it began. The asking became an important piece for me, a piece I couldn't recognize until less than a decade ago. Because something was taken from me without my permission, I began to conflate all forms of touch with someone taking something from me. In a way, that made sense—after all, good versions of touch are supposed to be healthy both in their giving *and* their reception simultaneously. But in my case, the touch hadn't been healthy—it was taken, not given. I began to steel myself against the coffee-breathed kisses of my dad, the beer-battered hugs of my grandfather, the cigarette-soaked kisses of one uncle, the cologne-scented hugs of another uncle, and the touch of any teen boy with the musk of dirty socks, Old Spice, and weed.

The only adult male I welcomed a hug from was my horse-farming-construction-working uncle who always smelled of sweat and earth, horse manure and hard work, with a tinge of red wine. His touch I trusted. As I grew, I would add more and more people to the list of those I trusted with touch, but I treated many as if they had to earn it.

Finding and Dodging Trusted Touch as a Young Adult

The list of those I trusted grew when I had my first kiss at age thirteen. I had never heard the terminology "heavy petting" until my family ventured into the most conservative ilk at the time—the homeschool culture of the 1990s—but my middle school boyfriend and I took that phrase to its most intimate levels using a different terminology. He laughed at me for not knowing what first, second, or third base were, and then introduced me to all three of them one week when our families were vacationing together. That we remained virgins in the technical sense is a miracle to me.

Like most middle school romances, we lasted only a few weeks, after which we didn't talk for months until he sent a letter to me expressing how sorry he was for his actions. Somehow it never occurred to me that I also owed him an apology. Though we were both young and I was certainly impressionable, he didn't "take advantage of me" against my will. Yes, our touch was immature and wrong. And yes, neither of us knew the long-term consequences of what we were doing. But we didn't know at thirteen years old that legally speaking, minors aren't considered able to give consent. As far as we both knew, this experience was mutual in every way. He was the introducer of the sin, but I eagerly took part, interested in it, wanting to go along. Though many young teen girls may have been uncomfortable or fought off the advances of this boy had they been in my shoes, I didn't. I liked it, and I was just as culpable for our actions.

That brief middle-school romance awakened something in me. It awakens in all of us at some point, I suppose, but in our fumbling hands and hot breaths under his sleeping bag, I had experienced my first orgasm and it was electrifying, terrifying, and addicting. I was naive enough to think this strange jolt of pleasure was going to result in pregnancy. I nearly held my breath until my next period, crying with relief when it finally came.

This began a years-long battle with masturbation and a history of either no touch at all with boyfriends or the opposite—nearly unhindered touch. I was unable to remain ambivalent about touch.

※ ※ ※

Around this time, I met the girl who has been my closest friend ever since. We were neighbors and we became insepa-rable. My own home was brimming with the male anatomy, but here, in her, was my likeness, my mirror. For the first time in my life I was fully comfortable with my body. There was never anything erotic in our love for one another. It was simply the beauty of commonality, something I'd never before experienced.

We would sleep squeezed against one another in her slanted ceiling bedroom at night, staring at the plastic glow-in-the-dark star constellations above us. We would hold hands while we walked or talked, and hug every time we saw one another, which was every day. We thought nothing of changing in front of one another, using the bathroom in front of one another, or jumping into or out of the shower while the other was there. My body was comfortable with her. Fully. Completely. Not inappropriately. Not sexually. Simply the experience of being.

When I was eighteen, my family moved six hours north of our childhood home and, shortly after, one of my younger brothers was killed suddenly in an accident. My childhood friend was on my family's doorstep as quickly as possible, and while I woke weeping all night long that first night, her body curved at my back, her hand brushed my sweaty hair back and her fingers tracked my tears down my face. This kind of selfless love was and still continues to be astounding to me. Besides my husband, she is still the one with whom I am most comfortable physically. She knows me completely and loves me. When we grew up she became a massage therapist, and she still gives more freely of her touch than anyone I have ever known—there is a strange kind of purity in it. It is one of the most profound expressions of *phileo*, brotherly love.[2] Familial love.

In this moment of agony, I needed human contact. This is something I think Jesus understands about mourning. Though my ailment at the time was not blindness, this friend's actions reminded me of Jesus when He healed the blind men in Matthew 20:29–34. When He sees their distress, their utter brokenness, and their inability to comfort or heal themselves, He doesn't pray for them from afar or simply yell "be healed!" from the other side of the room. Instead, we're told that "moved with compassion, Jesus *touched* their eyes."[3] When Jesus is undone over human suffering, He comes close and He touches. Yes, His moments of healing were not just one-off instances of compassion; they were pointing to the nature of God's Kingdom that was afoot. When He touched and healed, it wasn't for mere show—it was pointing to

---

[2] John 11:3.
[3] Matthew 20:34.

something much greater. But still, when moved with compassion, Jesus *touched*. And He usually touches in the particular place of pain or lack—for these men, it was their eyes. In suffering, Jesus gets closer than a family member would, but in the purest of ways. As I look back, I can see this is the type of compassion my friend displayed for me.

❈ ❈ ❈

I had boyfriends throughout my teens and twenties, but the relationships weren't very affectionate. After all, I was the product of a conservative homeschool culture, aged fifteen when the bestseller *I Kissed Dating Goodbye* was released. It turns out, if you read that book, you didn't only kiss dating goodbye, you kissed kissing goodbye too. In fact, there was a collective fear of *any* kind of physical touch in *any* relationship before marriage within our purity culture. And, like every good product of legalism, we took everything to the extreme. This meant most of my relationships were short-lived, secretive, or so physically restrained we could barely brush shoulders with one another without feeling guilty.

In my early twenties, my most serious boyfriend and I couldn't figure out why we made such great friends but couldn't make all the love stuff materialize. I look back now (with no regrets) and see why. We barely touched one another. I was terrified of "giving my heart away"[4] in the form

---

[4] A popular phrase we used in talking about relationships, and one I've found that many people use, though I cannot find an original source for it.

of holding hands. He was unwilling to "awaken love until the appropriate time"[5] in the form of small kisses or caresses. So our entire relationship was made up of delight and deep conversations and an unbelievably deep fear of expressing our affection for one another in a physical way.

Meanwhile, the trust of touch I had lost as a child was in many ways revived, and my brotherly love for everyone else in my life—male and female—was effusive. I was known for my warm touch; my mom's gift of giving enveloping hugs had been imparted to me and now my hugs even had their own nickname: "Lore Hugs." Yet in the relationship I cared most about (my boyfriend's and mine), I withheld touch completely. Most of my future dating relationships would follow the same system of thought and practice.

Confidence and Confusion in My Twenties

I had moved out of my parents' home shortly after my younger brother was killed and my youngest brother (the two-pound preemie) was born. This began a stint of living with over thirty-eight different roommates until marriage. Thirty-eight different women in various stages and stations of life. Some worked full time, some worked three jobs, some were in college, some in graduate school, some were in recovery, some weren't believers, some were my best friends, some felt like a blip on my life radar. But all of them mark my years of singleness.

---

[5] Song of Solomon 8:4.

Something happens when we live in long seasons of singleness: Many of us begin to feel starved of good, healthy, edifying touch. I wasn't living with family anymore. And I wasn't in middle school anymore, squeezing together on a twin bed with my best friend at night talking about dreams and boys under glow-in-the-dark stars. I've never had that kind of relationship with another friend. But with all these roommates, I knew healthy touch had to be possible and good. I made it my aim to welcome the human need for physical touch among my roommates and engage my own felt need.

I had no idea that what seemed like healthy familial touch for me (someone who came from a roughhousing household) could be a land mine for someone else.

A back rub, sitting close on the couch while watching a movie, spending the night at the other's house, sitting on the other's lap playfully—all these behaviors were common in the all-female houses in which I lived for fourteen years as a single person. We were effusively physical with one another. No one ever said it was inappropriate and I think we would have laughed if anyone had said it, and just snuggled more. We were the same gender, after all, and since touch with boys was *off limits*, who else were we supposed to touch and who was supposed to touch us?

The Purity culture of the '80s and '90s bred the physicality of same-gender friendship among my millennial friends. Our touch seemed platonic, good, familial, healthy, even necessary. We weren't receiving healthy, warm, and biblical forms of touch from anyone else—parents, brothers, pastors, and so on—so we were forced to find it in each other. It was the only place a human could touch another human without suspicion. To feel "turned on" by this kind of touch among same-gender friends would have been absolutely foreign to most of us. That is, until it happened to one of us. And then it was happening everywhere.

In my late twenties and on into my thirties, woman after woman after woman would come to me in tears, confessing what they had thought was healthy physical touch among same-gender friends had turned into something strangely sexual, and now many of them wondered if they were lesbians. They were all saying many of the same things: *we were just watching a movie and then . . . , we were just scratching each other's backs and then . . . , it was late and I stayed overnight and then . . .*

Shame was written in the faces of these women, most of whom had spent their adolescent, teen, and college years dreaming of boyfriends, husbands, and babies, not wondering if they were attracted to their own gender. And yet, here they were, feeling the chemical rush of endorphins and oxytocin that happens when we touch another human intimately. They were thrust into a confusing existential crisis because the one area of touch that seemed okay, permissible, and safe for a good, Christian girl, was bringing on feelings they never would have entertained before. Feelings they only associated with illicit touch because it elicited *feeling*—they felt *felt*. And they assumed feeling felt must be wrong.

If touching our same gender could lead to this, was there any place touching wasn't troublesome?

As I headed into my late twenties, I found the reluctance of touching boyfriends begin to creep over in touch toward almost all men in general. I felt uncomfortable with the touch of pastors, professors, ministers, father-figures, and brothers—and not necessarily because I was uncomfortable, but because they seemed to be. I couldn't explain why then, but looking back, I know it's because I had a growing awareness that the female body was somehow a possible threat. Not in the way my thirteen-year-old body had been with another thirteen-year-old boy, or in the way I'd been abused as a child, but in a, *"Danger, keep away!"* way, and this time *I* was the danger.

I was watching women fall into affairs with ministers, pastors fall into sin and lose their ministry, and men I trusted as father-figures seem a bit creepy with their touch toward my friends. We were women with burgeoning bodies, suddenly comfortable with who we were, no longer awkward or uncomfortable college students trying on different masks for size and fit. Our confidence was attractive to men and somehow terrifying to them at the same time. We'd been sold a lie that men couldn't control their animalistic lust so women were the real problem, the prey who had to protect themselves *and* the predator. I had no idea at the time that human females weren't made by God as animalistic prey, and human males were not made by God as animalistic predators. I didn't understand that the sexes were not beasts, but instead, image-bearing *women* and *men*. And those are totally different categories.

I began to view myself as a threat because that's how I felt men perceived me. I didn't feel like a threat. I felt like a person, a human, a woman. I had breasts, yes, legs, thighs, a laugh, and a personality. I felt like a whole person, but I also felt like there was no middle road between a forced front hug with a man I didn't know or a quick, awkward side hug from a pastor or male friend I'd known half my life. It seemed like the ones with whom I shouldn't have been a threat saw me as such. And the ones who knew nothing about me thought nothing of squeezing me toward themselves in a locking grip from which I couldn't escape or breathe. It seemed like my ability to control who touched me and how, was gone. Human touch felt backwards to me—not touching those closest to me, and at the same time, being forced to touch those who had just met me. Bear hugs were happening in introductory conversations with strangers, but were off-limits to those who were like my brothers. It was as though I was an inadvertent threat by nature of my gender or a forced participant in a touching game I didn't want to play.

Two Engagements and One Marriage in My Thirties

In my 32nd year, I began dating and quickly got engaged to a man I'd known for several years. Even as I look back now, I'm still confused as to what was going on in my heart and mind during that time. There weren't a lot of physical boundaries with us—I was intent on throwing off the legalistic tendencies of my teens and twenties, and felt no guilt about kissing. He hadn't had a girlfriend in fifteen years and I think the newness of it all got to both of us. Our engagement lasted a few months before I called it off. No matter how hard I tried, I couldn't obtain the mysterious sense of certainty my married friends seemed to have had about their spouses, and I wanted it. I was a child of divorce and knew marriage could be hard, yet meant for a lifetime, I wanted to know that I knew that I knew. And I didn't know.

There was also sometimes an element of lust on my behalf with him that I couldn't reconcile with the love I knew I was meant to have for a husband. I wanted to be touched and kissed, and being touched felt like taking a long, deep drink from an endless well. I just didn't want to be touched by *him*. And I hated this about myself. It was one of the most humbling years of my life, coming face-to-face with my own sins, lusts, fears, insecurities, disappointments, and more.

This man's touch, though, awakened a realization in me, and it wasn't just lust. It was the realization that it was possible to touch as an unmarried couple without losing your virginity. This reality seemed to buck the Purity Movement's main message: touch before marriage was always likened to a car drifting downhill, impossible to stop. One second you're just holding hands and the next you're having the best sex of your life. In this relationship, though, I learned it was possible to show restraint and respect, to say, "Wait. This isn't honoring you or me. Let's redirect our attention." I learned touch could not only be permissible within dating, but also truly good, helpful, healing, and even holy. Yes, as is with any kind of relationship, there were impure motives and moments. But on the whole, as it relates to the physical moments of our relationship, I can say we operated in purity, discernment, and self-control. We were able to be both *affectionate* and *Spirit-led*, two things I once thought were mutually exclusive.

Even as I still wrestled with the public shame of a broken engagement and lost relationship, I had no idea that God was about to usher me into that beautiful certainty I desired.

※ ※ ※

On an autumn evening, I met my husband-to-be in our church's foyer and it was a non-event for both of us. I have no recollection of our conversation. Nate remembers I had just gotten home from a trip to New York[6] and New England, and another trip, this time to Israel, was on the horizon. He was at the end of a long season of waiting and reflection after his divorce was finalized. He and his former wife

---

[6] I realize I'm mentioning a lot of different geographic locations where I lived at various junctures of this story. Just to help you, reader: From 1980–1998, I lived in Bucks County, Pennsylvania, a suburb of Philadelphia. From 1999–2003, I lived in Potsdam, New York, on the outskirts of the Adirondack Mountain region. In 2003, I spent most of the year living in Central America teaching English, and then moved back to Potsdam, New York, until 2005, when I moved to Chattanooga, Tennessee, to finish my degree in English. After I graduated in 2007, I moved back to Potsdam, and lived there until 2009, when I moved to the Dallas-Fort Worth Metro area. I lived in Texas, until the evening of my wedding, when we moved to Denver, Colorado, where I was on staff at a church there, and then had to suddenly move to Washington, D.C., for my husband's position with the United States Postal Service Headquarters. After a year in D.C., we returned to Texas. If you're keeping count, that's ten cross-country (or global) moves.

had been separated for a few years at that point and, though there were biblical grounds for their divorce, he had signed the papers in grief. On top of the emotional and spiritual loss he was undergoing, he was also learning what it meant to go without the kind of sexual touch in marriage he had grown accustomed to for twelve years. Nate describes that time as "white-knuckling it at first, followed by a sweet time with the Lord where He revealed He was enough."

We went on our first date six months after meeting. Three months later to the day, we were married. I imagine those who had watched me get engaged quickly the year before were probably shocked we moved that quickly. But we were surrounded by our closest friends, cheers from all, and the abundant blessing of our church and pastors, along with the certainty that we knew that we *knew* it was the right thing.

Nate led in dating and engagement with purity, showing restraint at every step, and caring for my body as though it was not his, or even mine, but God's. We married quickly partially because we knew we were going to get married and exercising physical restraint was difficult, but also simply because we could. Our engagement was just long enough to do the required premarital counseling with our dear friends, an elder and his wife from our church who would marry us. It was no longer than that on purpose. We knew our desire for one another was pure and without lust, but we didn't want the enemy to get a foothold in our pure desire. We tried to be aware of our sinful propensities and set boundaries for them.

We joke about it now, but Nate's vehicle, a VW Touareg, had so many different alarms and beeps. One for unbuckled seat belts, one for when the weight shifted on the passenger seat, one for if the car was running too long without seat-belts buckled in—and none of them stopped. It was June in Texas and turning the car off while we kissed wasn't an option for the 100-degree weather. So when the annoying beeps interrupted us, we called it a move of the Holy Spirit and thanked God. Even though we were thirty-four and thirty-eight, we wanted to see things like the car, the presence of roommates in both of our lives, self-imposed curfews, or other restraints, as God's provision for us against taking a gift before its time. Contrary to what some seem to suggest, Christians never get to an age where we somehow grow out of needing to obey God's design for sexual experiences. Age is never an excuse for disobedience.

Only by God's grace were we able to get to marriage not having had sex with one another. I phrase it that way on purpose. It is only ever by God's grace that anyone comes to marriage a virgin or is able to show restraint with their fiancé. I'm grateful that God took me on a very specific journey before marriage, where He showed me my sins of selfishness and lust, taught me to be restrained, and yet only brought me through singleness by His grace alone. Virginity wasn't the prize I gave my husband on our wedding night, and sex wasn't the prize he gave me—all of it was grace, grace, grace.

Married but Mismatched

Right after we were married we were the stereotypical new couple in some ways, holding hands, standing close, having a lot of sex (although in many marriages, this experience isn't as common as most people expect it to be). All my years of being untouched now culminated in this new marriage where touch was both beneficial and permitted. There was one problem though: my husband didn't love physical touch as much as I did. Any kind of physical touch in public seemed to make him uncomfortable. He was never rough about it, but he'd pull his arm away if it tickled or turn his head away if he didn't want me to touch his beard. Nor did he offer touch in private often or enthusiastically. I'd ask for a back-scratch or massage and he'd do it half-heartedly for a few minutes and then stop. He was generous with his touch if we were moving toward sexual intimacy, but during the monotony of the day, he was stingy with affection and I was starving.

I felt confused. Wasn't this supposed to be the wide pasture of marriage? Touch wasn't off-limits now, so why did it seem to be such a tender thing? Was he embarrassed by me in public? Didn't he want to be seen touching me?

I had believed that marriage was the one place touch would be unhindered. Yet Nate believed physical touch was always sexual in nature and didn't have a box for touch that wasn't foreplay leading to sex. His family, though stable and dear, was not physically affectionate when he was growing up and his previous marriage hadn't been either. Touch was reserved for sex.

My experience with touch, though, had mostly only ever been for companionship. I was free with my touch, not only with him, but with other brothers and sisters in appropriate ways. He would say he was awkward with it. He had just learned to practice intimacy with men within the past few years in terms of confession, accountability, and good, honest hugging. He barely knew how to hug a woman without it being quick, clean, and from the side, if he hugged at all. He wanted to learn and grow in these areas (and he did, quickly!), and I wanted to grow in respecting his comfort level for touch, but it took a lot of communication between the two of us about what we liked and didn't. Why we thought public affection was good or awkward. Why we felt a need to be touched or not touched in certain ways at certain times. I had to learn that although we were one flesh, he was still my brother and neighbor in Christ and a human with different preferences than me. He had a sensitivity to all touch, in fact, not limited to human or mine specifically, but even to fabric he didn't like or a clothing fit in which he didn't feel comfortable. And he had to learn that although we are one flesh, I was still his sister and neighbor in Christ, and a human with different desires than him. For me, that meant a high desire for physical closeness, frequent and varied kinds of touching—most of which were not related to sex at all.

The Story You Are Living

This is my story up to present day. All of this has formed me and how I view, use, and receive touch from others. But touch is an infinitely complicated thing. Just small slivers of my story show how complex, layered, and difficult it is to navigate. I am a northerner writing this from Texas. I was single for thirty-four years and now I am married. I am a wife but not a mother of living children. I am a sister of only brothers. I have been sexually abused. My parents are divorced. I am an introvert. I have very few close friends but many, many acquaintances. Those are the things I bring with me to this topic, but you probably bring a whole different history with you. My story is complicated differently than your story.

You're a pastor. You're a pastor's wife. You're single. You live in the city. You are a college student. You have a disability. You are a mother of many. You are a father of none. You have many siblings. Your family is small. You have a sexual history. You've never kissed anyone. You have been abused. You have been raped. You have been loved. You hate hugs. You hug everyone. You spank your kids. You loathe corporeal punishment of any kind. The list of what makes your experiences unique could go on and on.

Your story is infinitely complex and different than mine, and this one book can't give answers to the complicated stories, narratives, and journeys we're all on with touch. For me to give you a list of to-dos or never-dos regarding touch would be to fail from the onset. So, in the rest of this book, as I've said before, I will not be giving you how-tos regarding touch. It will never be my aim to give ten steps to touching or tips for touching appropriately. If you finish this book and that's what you've gotten, I've failed. If you picked up this book looking for that, please know right now, I won't give it to you. My aim again and again will be to show you to the grandness of God, His love for you, His love for others, and how that should *inform* how you *think* about and practice touch. My goal is to broaden the pastures of touch in which you run.

My ultimate goal is this: I want to make you *think* about how you touch, who you touch, why you touch, where you touch, when you touch, and what you touch—but never to *tell* you how, who, why, where, when, or what to touch. As Paul David Tripp says, "We cannot simply offer people a system or give advice on how to deal with their past. We must point them to a powerful and present Redeemer. *He* is our only hope."[7] My aim is to point you to Christ and implore you to think about how He was touched and touched others, and to allow His actions and His love for you to bear weight on how you give and receive touch.

In many ways the following chapters will be a mere primer on touch, meant to raise questions without completely answering them, to offer wisdom and general guidance, but not necessarily specific guidelines. My intention is to simply begin a conversation that you take back with you into your life and your faith community to consider, evaluate, and grow in together.

I get my take on touch from Scripture itself, and though there are clear lines in some places, more often the Bible offers us more of a descriptive look at touch than a prescriptive

---

[7] Paul David Tripp, *Instruments in the Redeemer's Hands* (Phillipsburg, NJ: P&R Publishing, 2002), 12.

outline for each and every scenario we find ourselves in. Just as there are many descriptive portions of Scripture that we can discern as accounts of sin (slavery, polygamy, incest, etc.), so will there be biblical descriptions of touch that we must take the time and care to morally discern as well. This means we must choose to walk in humility, trusting the Holy Spirit to give us wisdom when we ask, discernment when we're confused, healing when we need it, forgiveness for where we've sinned, and help for all the ways we use our hands to live.

We are all going to have to walk carefully among these ideas. I hope after reading this, you (and I, as I do the seemingly impossible task of unearthing some lies and trying to find some redemption) will be able to think more clearly about the complication of touch, the beauty of it, the need for it, and the ministry of it.

CHAPTER TWO

Speaking the Same (Love) Language

You can't change your fingerprints.
You have only ten of them. And you
leave them on everything you touch;
they are definitely not a secret.[1]
—Al Franken

W hen I was growing up, my parents were big fans of road trips. With a family as large as ours, flights weren't an option. We'd all pile into the station wagon, the van, or the red Ford Fiesta. I have distinct memories of the floor of that Fiesta. It was so rusted out, my dad lined it with flattened cardboard boxes and newspapers to keep us from falling

---

[1] Alice Truong, "Senator Al Franken Wrote Tim Cook a Letter: What's the Deal with Touch ID?" *Fast Company*, September 20, 2013.

through (this was 1983, and things were a little more lax back then). As I previously mentioned, we were a tactile family, touching one another constantly. When things got out of hand, playfully or roughly, my mom would turn around and say firmly, "If you can't keep your hands to yourself—or if you don't know what to do with them—I'm going to make you sit on them."

This time-out to consider the way we were touching each other was to teach us restraint, and maybe this is what our world needs a little of right now, a time-out to think. Because things have gotten out of hand in the church, and in culture at large too.

Selfishness in the Church

There's a pervasive belief in the church, popularized by the bestselling book series *The Five Love Languages*, that we give and receive love in five ways—quality time, acts of service, words of affirmation, gift-giving, and physical touch. Author Gary Chapman's point in the series is not merely to identify one's own "love language," but to teach us how to serve others by showing them love in the language of love they receive best. This understanding has done much good in many marriages and families, I'm sure. The book helps me understand why there are certain needs around me that I notice and meet reflexively, and why there are other needs around me that I overlook and do not meet because I feel incapable or "not wired that way." Chapman's work in this arena is helpful for those, like me, who are unlikely to meet needs outside their comfort zone.

The unfortunate thing, though, is many Christians use Chapman's categories for the opposite reason he offers them in the first place. Though his goal is to help us give love to others in a language they best receive it, the church, as I've noticed, uses his categories to neglect the expressions of love they should be offering others. Instead of giving love in the language another would receive it best, I've heard many Christians say, "But that's not my love language" as their unchallengeable excuse for refusing to offer love. So when it comes to touch, if one doesn't naturally want to offer physical contact in appropriate contexts that they probably should, they can use the tidy excuse of love language. Or conversely, if someone wants to receive—or sinfully take—touch from another, they can use the love-language lingo as a manipulative bartering chip for their demands.

Another way the love-language paradigm is misused is that it can easily operate off the mentality of, "If I scratch your back, you'll tend to scratch mine. If you're happy to see me, I'll tend to be happy to see you, too," as David Powlison notes.[2] Powlison is pointing out the self-centeredness inherent in much of our language about love, and therefore touch. A well-intentioned paradigm was created for us to give love, and we have hijacked it and made it all about receiving.

The apostle Paul had some strong words about our actions being more about receiving than giving. In Acts 20:35, he

---

[2] David Powlison, "Love Speaks Many Languages Fluently," *Journal of Biblical Counseling* (Fall 2002).

points out that "it is necessary to help the weak by laboring like this and to remember the words of the Lord Jesus, because he said, 'It is more blessed to give than to receive.'" When we knowingly withhold love from another *in the way they receive it best*, we expose that we think more highly of ourselves than the person we should be loving. When we concern ourselves more with how serving another will eventually help *us* than how serving another will help *them*—well, this is the root of a whole host of sins.

A lot of times in the church, our language and motivation around love and touch, and therefore our actions, lean most toward selfishness, self-protection, and selfish gain. Even with good tools for loving others in our hands, like Chapman's book and others, we turn the tools inward and make everything about self.

Confusion in the Culture

Motivation for love and touch isn't only broken in the church, it's broken in culture, too. On October 15, 2017, a hashtag was used on social media at noon. By the end of the day, it had been used 200,000 times, and by the following day it was tweeted more than 500,000 times. When it comes to the usage on Facebook, "the hashtag was used by more than 4.7 million people in 12 million posts during the first 24 hours."[3]

---

[3] Wikipedia contributors, "The MeToo Movement," *Wikipedia, The Free Encyclopedia,* https://en.wikipedia.org/wiki/Me_Too_movement (accessed June 17, 2019).

The hashtag was #metoo. Celebrities, authors, teachers, actors, teenagers, employees, employers, politicians, singles, stay-at-home moms, wives, sisters, and people from every walk of life, every ethnicity, and every age were using it to say they too had been on the receiving end of unwelcomed, inappropriate touch, words, or other actions. I used it too, briefly sharing of times I was touched inappropriately by a coworker who would always follow it up by saying, "I'm just kidding! Can't you take a joke?" And in this very book, I've told you about when I was sexually abused as a child.

The #metoo movement brought to light all kinds of sexual harassment and abuse by those who, in most cases, assumed their actions were either welcomed, only playful, or were owed in some way.[4] Our culture stands in the landmark moment of a war that has been silently borne by women for generations.

But we are in another landmark moment as well. In the same autumn of 2017, when the #metoo hashtag took the world by storm, a movie was released and nominated for multiple Academy Awards. *Call Me by Your Name* is the story of a twenty-four-year-old man who woos and wins the affections of a seventeen-year-old boy. The movie received rave reviews and three Academy Award nominations. While the world was raging over all kinds of inappropriate sexual acts toward employers and their employees, teachers and their students, youth pastors and kids in their youth groups, culture was also

---

[4] The #metoo movement has also been cited as beginning by Tarana Burke, African American Civil Rights Activist, who began using the phrase in 2006.

raving over this movie glorifying a relationship between an adult and a minor that, if it wasn't fiction, would mean jail time and cultural shunning from every side.

What a confusing time in which to live.

When we don't understand the healthy expression of something, or the innate purpose of it, and when it is shrouded in mystery, we don't know what to do but invent, pervert, or usurp it in every way. This is why we find the same people using #metoo one day, only to celebrate a film that encourages violations of consent and age the next. The same could be said for the exploitation of women—in one moment, our society demands equal dignity for women in the public square, and the next, it gives all its money to industries that require them to undress in order to make it. Our society simply doesn't know what to do with the human body or human touch. Our culture is confused, and confusion only results in more confusion.

Learning the Language of Care

Culture is telling itself lies about touch. It tells them in films, in music, on beaches and in boardrooms, in marriages and in schools. And the church is telling itself lies about touch too. For example, in some churches, the lies can sound like this: We should hold one another at arm's length to "avoid the appearance of evil," or we should barely side-hug the opposite gender, presupposing everyone we hug has ill motives. In other churches, the lie may sound like this: Though we've been commanded in the Bible to warmly receive one another, our lack of physical touch between brothers and sisters in Christ is excusable, and can be chalked up to "that not being our love language."

Here's the thing though: though the lies abound, most of us really do want to use touch in good and godly ways. We see that touch matters, but we simply don't know what to do with it. On one side of the spectrum, we lament the effects of the purity culture that has come before us—which views touch as something to be completely withheld or avoided. On the other side of the spectrum, we lament with the victims of the #metoo movement—whose abusers view touch as something to be forcefully taken. None of us wants to live in either extreme, so we become like the fidgeting child in the backseat during a long road-trip, not knowing what to do with our hands.

When we look at the polarized options for touch these days, we could easily run away from the issue altogether in fear of making a mistake in either direction. But one of the greatest errors in our moment in history will be if we let this moment pass us by without a better understanding and practice of healthy, pure, good touch. On a national level, the topic of touch is on the table now—both in the public square and in the church. We have a unique chance to embody a godly, caring approach to this issue that neither withholds touch, nor forcefully takes it. And the key word there is *caring*. We need to teach how to touch with true *care*. Care for our own bodies and for the bodies of others, because those bodies were created by a good and caring God. If we don't know what to do with our hands or can't keep them to ourselves, the answer isn't to sit on them for all of time. It's to learn to use them rightly—and to train our sons and daughters from a young age the practice of caring touch.

※ ※ ※

In order for us to learn to use touch rightly, a couple things are required.

First, we have to understand that touch itself—as well as all the things we touch—is from God. Though touch should be important for everyone, its importance should be especially clear for believers because our God made a touchable, material world. And He made humans within that world with five senses to purposefully engage it.

Second, we have to understand that none of us are free from the effects of sin on this world, and what we do with our bodies *matters*. We are born with fallenness and brokenness woven through our very being, and, at the same time, our bodies are also becoming a history in themselves. This means we are both carriers of brokenness in terms of our physical family history *and* our spiritual family history, and we also engage in creating both more brokenness *and* more beauty as we live. We are both singular and corporate, and so our actions have individual repercussions as well as communal ones.

Third, using touch rightly requires *thinking* about touch rightly, and that means recognizing its nuanced complexity. One contributor to this complexity is language. We've all witnessed conversations where two people were using the same word, but in their minds, the definition of that word was not the same. We do the same thing with the language of our bodies—we use words that largely do not have an agreed upon definition, thus constructive conversations about touch are almost impossible to achieve. As David Powlison would say, the language of the speaker needs to line up with the language of the hearer, and if it doesn't, well-meaning communication won't translate as care the way it's supposed to.[5]

Another contributor to the complexity of touch is social context. We don't simply bring our definitions; we also bring our family history, personal history, emotional history, and more. When David Linden was interviewed about his book *Touch*, he summed it up well: "The sensory experience of touch can't be divorced from the emotional experience, he explained, because the way humans perceive touch depends on its social context. An arm thrown over your shoulders by a domineering boss is perceived very differently than an arm thrown around your shoulders by a trusted friend, for example. 'The sensation is perceived differently because the emotional touch centers in the brain are receiving signals about social nuances, even if the touching is identical.'"[6]

---

[5] David Powlison, "Love Speaks Many Languages Fluently," *Journal of Biblical Counseling* (Fall 2002), https://mattadair.typepad.com /communitas/files/five_love_languages_critique.pdf.
[6] Jessica Lahey, "Should Teachers Be Allowed to Touch Students?" *The Atlantic*, January 23, 2015, https://www.theatlantic.com/education /archive/2015/01/the-benefits-of-touch/384706/?fbclid=IwAR1W_dRJ YVKN1wBeX7DGkbHh1FLrwQvyRh15jV20p34gThS9O0y0eMMT 8_Y.

For people who have been assaulted or abused, the way they understand and perceive a pastoral hug may be vastly different than others who have never been harmed by an authority figure. And then, even among those who have been assaulted, experiences differ. If an abused woman has seen justice served against her perpetrator and has had time to process her experience, she may be more open to an appropriate pastoral hug or hand on the shoulder. But another abused woman who has not seen justice restored, or is perhaps still fighting the lie that her personhood is the equivalent of a sexual object, may recoil from such a touch. It might be the same pastoral touch from the same man, but different people will have vastly different readings of his intentions. This is why touch is such a landmine in the Church and world, and requires great discernment. We're all operating from different perspectives with different intentions. Touch is so informed by our stories, histories, vocations, and stations that a working understanding of the categories of touch will be helpful.

Categories of Touch

There are three main categories of touch—platonic, sexual, and professional. Within each of these categories there is a distinction between healthy *giving* of touch and a healthy *receiving* of touch. (These are not to be confused with an unhealthy *forced* touch or an unhealthy *taken* touch). While most of us do not have a hard time understanding the categories or *kinds* of touch (after all, most of us know intrinsically it's not right to touch someone sexually in a professional setting), it seems our confusion lies in the ways we should give and receive touch within each category (one can intend to give touch in one way while it is being received an entirely different way).

Here I will define healthy touch as "ministering" and unhealthy touch as "sinful." I want to convey that all touch, giving and receiving, has the potential to be either healthy (ministering) or unhealthy (sinful). Just as there's death and life in the power of the tongue, there is death and life in the power of the touch.

Platonic Touch: This is touch that is "free from sensual desire, especially in a relationship between two persons of the opposite sex."[7] Or, I'll add, between two persons free from sexual desire. This is the kind of touch we see most commonly within families or between close friends.

1. *Giving* Ministering Platonic Touch: Giving ministering platonic touch will be touch that aims to serve the person to whom we give it. It will be for their good, to calm them, help heal them, show them we love them, and they are safe with us. It does not incite sexual feelings or feelings of being powerful or dominating. If it does, it is no longer ministering platonic touch.

2. *Receiving* Ministering Healthy Platonic Touch: Receiving ministering platonic touch from someone with whom we are in relationship (friend or family) will comfort us, soothe us, remind us we are loved. It should not incite sexual feelings or feelings of being violated. These are

---

7 Platonic. 2019. Retrieved December 7, 2018 from https://www.dic tionary.com/browse/platonic.

touch-experiences in which *both* individuals do not intend to incite or receive sexual pleasure.

3. *Taking* Sinful Platonic Touch: Taking sinful platonic touch is any touch with the intention to hold power over or dominate the person we are touching. It is not with care for the other, but a selfish desire to assert one's own body over the body of the other. This is abuse, and God hates abuse.

4. *Feeling* Sinful Platonic Touch: Feeling touched in sinful platonic ways should free the one who is being touched to remove themselves from the situation if they are able. If it is abuse, the one abused may need to report the abuser to authorities.

Sexual Touch: This is touch where there is physical attraction from one or both parties involved. It is not always reciprocated, and therefore it's the one most rife with confusion. Generally defined, it relates to "the instincts, physiological processes, and activities connected with physical attraction or intimate physical contact between individuals."[8] It belongs primarily between a husband and wife.[9]

1. *Giving* Ministering Sexual Touch: Giving sexual touch that is ministering focuses on the other person. It will be in search of the other's pleasure, and aim to serve their physical needs or desires within the good confines of sex as God designed it, between a husband and wife. Its goal should be intimacy, connection, enjoyment, and sometimes, procreation. And as obvious as this may sound, it bears saying: both

---

[8] Sexual. 2019. Retrieved May 20, 2019 from https://www.lexico.com/en/definition/sexual.

[9] Genesis 2:24–25; Hebrews 13:4.

partners should be giving healthy sexual touch in their marriage, putting the other's experience before their own. There should not be a trend in which one party consistently gives healthy sexual touch and the other does not (an exception being if one has a physical disability).

A very important thing to note here is that not every physical interaction between spouses will be in the category of sexual touch. Many times, healthy forms of platonic touch should also happen within marriage, and when it doesn't, touch within marriage loses its robustness and holistic quality. When every physical encounter in a marriage is interpreted as sexual, both parties reduce the other to a pleasure object and not a complex human made in God's image with complex needs.

2. *Receiving* Ministering Sexual Touch: Receiving sexual touch that is ministering will always be safe within the good confines of marriage between a man and woman, and will always include permission to stop or ask for something different if someone is in pain or uncomfortable. It will not always result in peak sexual pleasure (an expectation promised in many Christian circles if one waits for marriage), but it should result in a sense of peace and rest in one another. Again, both partners should be receiving healthy sexual touch in their marriage. There should not be a trend in which one party consistently receives healthy sexual touch and the other does not (an exception being if one has a physically disability).

3. *Taking* Sinful Sexual Touch: Taking sexual touch that is sinful will be aimed toward self-pleasure, the domination of the other, or manipulation of others against their will. It

will not consider the other's desires or needs. It may not consider their safety or their future. Many times, it is outside the confines of marriage between a man and woman, and other times, it happens within marriages. It *always* harms. Sinfully taking sexual touch from another against their will is abuse, and God hates abuse.

4. *Feeling* Sinful Sexual Touch: No one should be made to feel sinful sexual touch. There is no such thing as good or right or biblical sinful sexual touch. If one is being touched sexually against their will, in a way that harms them, or in a way that degrades them, they should remove themselves if they're able (though most times in these cases, they are unable to remove themselves because they have been dominated by an abuser), seek safety, and report it to the authorities. This is important: if you are not undergoing sinful sexual touch, but know someone who is, you should help them get out of the situation, offer them safety, and call the proper authorities. This type of touch is abuse, and God hates abuse.

Before I go on, I'd like to offer a disclaimer: I am not an expert on sexual abuse, nor am I a counselor or a police officer. Because I lack the depth and scope of information that these types of people have, and because I'm addressing this topic quickly, I'd like to point you to a more thorough resource that will better equip you to deal with the topic of sexual abuse: churchcares.com.

Professional Touch: "Skilled healing touch given as part of a professional relationship between a client and therapist."[10] Though not all cases would use or require the terms "client" and "therapist," this category will include touch between anyone in a professional capacity and those to whom they are ministering or caring for. In *most* cases, the individuals involved would not be considered equal peers on the terms in which they meet; one of the two will be in the power seat. Though they may be on equal footing in terms of size, age, or gender, one will most likely be coming to the other in search of something they are unable to get on their own, like medical care, therapy, a job, or pastoral care. Therefore, the one doing the touching would likely be the one with the greater power, and the onus is on them to wield that power humbly, purely, and faithfully.

1. *Giving* Ministering Professional Touch: Giving ministering professional touch will always aim toward the other's emotional, physical, or spiritual healing, never their harm. Its end aim is always better function of the holistic self (body, mind, soul, spirit). In many cases (apart from a handshake) it should ask permission unless the situation is medical in nature, where the receiver has scheduled their appointment or needs immediate medical attention. (For example, when praying for someone or before hugging an unfamiliar person, I ask, "Is it okay if I hug you/lay a hand on your shoulder?")

2. *Receiving* Ministering Professional Touch: Receiving ministering professional touch should always result in feeling cared for and safe. Though at times it may *hurt*, its aim will always be to heal, as in the case of a doctor resetting a bone,

---

[10] Professional Touch. 2019. Retrieved May 20, 2019 from https://medical-dictionary.thefreedictionary.com/professional+touch.

or a massage therapist kneading out tight muscles, or a chiropractor adjusting a misaligned spine.

3. *Taking* Sinful Professional Touch: The taking of sinful professional touch will be any touch given from a professional to the other in a way that aims not to heal, but to harm, physically or sexually. It is gained by manipulation or force. It is abuse, and God hates abuse.

4. *Receiving* Sinful Unhealthy Professional Touch: The reception of sinful professional touch (if one can discern it is sinful as it's happening, which sadly, isn't usually the case) should always result in clear words from receiver to professional: "Don't do that." Or "No." Or "That makes me uncomfortable." If the words do not stop the touch, the receiver should remove themselves from the situation completely and report the experience to the professional's superior. If no official actions are taken at this point, the receiver should report the experience to the authorities. It is professional abuse, and God hates abuse.

Again, this disclaimer bears repeating: I am not an expert on sexual abuse, nor am I a counselor or a police officer. Because I lack the depth and scope of information that these types of people have, I'd like to point you to a resource that will better equip you to deal with the topic of sexual abuse: churchcares.com.

※ ※ ※

This is not an exhaustive definition of touch in all scenarios in all ways for all people. We will all need to contextualize touch in relationships in which we operate platonically, sexually, and professionally. And we also need to depend heavily and humbly on the Holy Spirit and the accountability of other believers to navigate touch in a healthy, ministering way. There is no rulebook for touch that isn't abuse. There's also no one who can tell the giver of touch how the other is receiving it except the one who is being touched. And there's no one who can assure the one being touched that the way she *feels* touched is not the way it's being intended. This is a difficult, difficult path to navigate because we are complex people, as I said, informed by our stories, histories, vocations, and stations. No one story is the same, and how one feels about being touched or touching cannot be assumed without communication.

Because many of us don't know what to do with our hands, we may be afraid to think about what *is* the *right* thing to do with them. In some ways there are clear laws, rights and wrongs. But in the more nebulous spaces, where we have to depend on the Spirit for discernment and guidance, or practice interpersonal skills we feel we lack, it can be terrifying to enter into a healthy practice of touch. Many of us just don't want to engage touch at all. Or perhaps we've been through trauma or have a disability that makes touch wildly uncomfortable for us. Or we fear misstepping around others who have undergone trauma or perhaps have a disability. We think it's easier to just leave it to others more comfortable with it. But as Zack Eswine would say, we have to push past those fears in the knowledge that "to love one's neighbor require[s] our close physical proximity."[11] Our neighbor doesn't need us to run away. As Jesus makes clear in the parable of the Good Samaritan, our neighbor needs us to come close and care for his wounds with our very hands.

This may feel uncomfortable for you, but I hope you'll read on. Allow the discomfort to reveal some things about yourself that you perhaps did not know, and also allow it to reveal others to you. Most of all, allow it to reveal who God has been and is to you. You don't have to come out on the other side loving touch or even convinced it's necessary. But my aim is to help us look at Jesus, and let the weight of His actions rest on ours. Eswine puts it clearly: "In order to navigate this rocky terrain we need an expert guide. Jesus is our expert guide. He is our compass for navigating the touch of the sick, the touch between men and women, and the touch of children."[12]

---

[11] Zack Eswine, *Sensing Jesus* (Wheaton, IL: Crossway, 2013), 179.
[12] Ibid., 183.

CHAPTER THREE

Broken Bloodlines

Lying, thinking
Last night
How to find my soul a home
Where water is not thirsty
And bread load is not stone
I came up with one thing
And I don't believe I'm wrong
That nobody,
But nobody
Can make it out here alone.[1]
—Maya Angelou

I spent some of my most formative years in a denomination with a high value on how one *felt* emotionally

---

[1] Maya Angelou, *The Poetry of Maya Angelou* (New York: Random House, 1993), 70.

about God. Our primary barometer for Christian health was whether we felt the emotion of joy in the presence of the Spirit and then how that emotion was expressed. Dancing, raising your hands, speaking in tongues, weeping in joy or gratitude, laughing—these seemed to be the expressed values by which our faith was measured.

On the cusp of my thirties, though, disillusioned with church as I experienced it, I found myself in the fresh air of a denomination that highly valued, instead, how one *thought* about God. Bible study was the thing. Learning to love the Lord our God with all our minds. Discussion. Inductive study. Being well read. All of these values began to take precedence in my Christian faith. They began to crowd out the emotive parts of my faith until there was hardly space for them anymore. I had been formed emotionally and now I was being formed intellectually. The result, for me, was a full mind and learned tongue, but anemic emotions and a lack of demonstrative worship toward God. I was like a bodybuilder who only ever worked out one side of his body: one arm bulging and strong, the other limp and weak.

I'm grateful for the exploration of the heart God created and the education of my mind with Scripture. But the thing is, I think what I equally needed during these years, sometimes even before the exercise of my emotions or intellect, was mostly just a hug.

Emotional and theological health is certainly important, and we shouldn't discount their necessity for full maturation in our faith. But it is not the moments of pure elation in the presence of the Spirit nor times of academic and theological clarity that stick out most in my mind as the way I came to not just *understand*, but truly *trust* in the assurance of God's love; it was the hugs. I can recall a few standout moments in my twenties and early thirties when I felt the joy of the Lord or the elation of understanding His Word, but mostly I remember the fatherly hug of my pastor in his backyard when I learned an awful truth about my family, the hand of a mother-figure brushing my hair back as I sobbed on her couch on a particularly painful and snowy Christmas evening, the embrace of a friend as she handed me cash for my car's new tires in a time I struggled financially, and the hug of a roommate after a disappointing date.

Those experiences are seared in my memory as moments I saw a glimpse of the gospel in flesh. They were good, pastoral, fatherly or motherly, brotherly or sisterly, hugs. It was the church acknowledging the humanness of it all, the tangible, touchable, brokenness of life, the confusion of doubt, the elation of joy, and the way these things were stored and felt in the body itself. It was John leaning back on Jesus to ask a question instead of yelling at Him from across the room (John 13:23). It was the Ephesian elders embracing Paul in sadness instead of keeping their distance (Acts 20:36–38). It was the brotherly affection Peter wishes for us (2 Pet. 1:7). Those moments for me were ministry, and they were pure.

I needed the touch of brothers and fathers and mothers and sisters to acknowledge that even though I felt alone, I was not alone. I needed the ministerial warmth of pastors, showing me my body was not a threat to them. I needed the enveloping hugs of older women, teaching me motherly figures could be trusted. I needed the affection of male peers to assure me our friendship was more important to them than their sexual desires. I needed the embrace of female peers to remember the friendship of God. We all need to remember the nearness of God in hard moments—and much of that comes in the form of life on the earth with other human beings who draw near to us.

But the church, apart from rare moments like the ones I just described, has not proven to be a safe, loving, or pure source for touch.

We make jokes about "side hugs" and "leaving room for the Holy Spirit" and "bromance." We set up strict boundaries around who we can touch, hug, or show physical familiarity with, and utilize strategic maneuvers to avoid embracing people well. We hold classes on appropriate touch for children's workers (which is needed, but unfortunate that this is our only context for talking about healthy touch with kids). We endlessly debate the helpfulness of practices like "The Billy Graham Rule" or the "Pence Rule." We advise women in abusive marriages to "stick them out" or, armed with a weak understanding of touch and its need, we suggest divorce to a spouse who doesn't like sex with their husband or wife. We hardly ever talk about sex candidly. In group settings, we shy away from subjects like masturbation, pornography, and sexting. We refuse to acknowledge sexual abuse when it does happen in our churches, many times deciding to handle it "in house" instead of taking it to the authorities. We give rules and principles and horror stories about pre-marital sex, and gloss over sex in pre-marital counseling sessions, hardly preparing couples who've remained chaste for the complexity of sex within marriage. We won't sit next to strangers at church, always leaving a spare chair between us and shirk when a stranger sitting beside us at church touches us accidentally.

We have it backwards in so many ways; we give a pass to horrible or even abusive forms of touch, while ignoring the gaping hole where good and godly types of touch should be—even when they are commanded of us in the Bible.

Word from the Beginning

I saw an exhibit of unfinished sculptures once. It was a room full of granite, wood, clay, and wire—all forms of something, but seemingly not the thing itself. Half faces, half bodies, well chiseled faces looking down at blocks for hands. While it appeared like half-finished art, it was this way on purpose. The sculptor intended them to look that way—as if fully-formed, intricate people were simply stepping out of raw material.

The exhibit reminded me of a story a friend told once about his grandfather whittling wood. "How do you know what it's going to be?" my friend asked him. "Well, son, this block of wood you see is an eagle. My job is just to take away all the parts that aren't eagle."

The sculpture's job is to interact with his creation, to form its shape and to bring it to completion as he sees it. It is to *touch*.

In Genesis 2:7, the Bible says, "Then the Lord God formed the man out of the dust." The stunning thing here is not only that man was made from dust, but that from dust he was *formed*. God gathered dust from the ground, mere particles, and touched them—formed them—into a man. Then in turn, He reached inside the man, taking his rib and from it formed a woman by His touch. In the other acts of creation—day and night; sun, moon, and stars; plants and animals—God *spoke* all things into existence. But in creating humankind, God chose His first act with man and woman to be touch, to use His hands. Why have we in the church diverged so far from His example?

Maybe we find our answer close by in the neighboring chapter. The first act of God was to touch and we quickly see the idea of touch distorted by Eve. The serpent came up to the woman and said, "Did God really say, 'You can't eat from any tree in the garden'?" Eve's reply? "We may eat the fruit from the trees in the garden. But about the fruit of the tree in the middle of the garden, God said, 'You must not eat it or *touch it*, or you will die.'"[2]

But God didn't say not to touch the tree.[3] He only said not to eat of it. We don't know if Adam passed on this altered message, or if Eve altered it due to her own fear, misunderstanding, or uncertainty. In any case, we know Eve added to the words of God, and we've been doing it in every area of life ever since. We call it wisdom in our arrogant moments and legalism in our honest ones. From the opening chapters of the

---

[2] Genesis 3:1–3, emphasis added.
[3] Genesis 2:16–17.

Bible, adding to what God has said about touch—and what Jesus and His followers practiced in the New Testament—hasn't produced less confusion in the church; it has produced more.

Legalism—adding extra parameters to God's Word—around touch is understandable. Abuse *is* rampant and affairs *are* commonplace. And touching others can be awkward—especially if we aren't sure they even want to be touched or if it will trigger unwanted feelings in them. But instead of moving toward people in our churches in appropriate ways, we move away from them in fear. But the abuse of a thing—or the awkwardness of it—doesn't make the thing itself bad or scary. Isn't that the logic we use with the Bible? Plenty of people have abused the Bible, twisting it to fit an agenda or pedaling it for profit. But that doesn't mean we should throw the Bible out in fear. It means we should use it rightly. The same goes for touch.

Wallace Stegner, in his Pulitzer Prize winning novel, *Angle of Repose*, wrote: "Touch. It is touch that is the deadliest enemy of chastity, loyalty, monogamy, gentility with its codes and conventions and restraints. By touch we are betrayed and betray others . . . an accidental brushing of shoulders or touching of hands . . . hands laid on shoulders in a gesture of comfort that lies like a thief, that took, not gave, that wanted, not offered, that awoke, not pacified. When one flesh is waiting, there is electricity in the merest contact."[4]

---

[4] Wallace Stegner, *Angle of Repose* (New York: Random House, 1971), 562.

"Electricity in the merest contact." Most of us have felt this electricity in contact with another's flesh, but because touch is so uncommon in our culture—and in the church—we immediately associate the electricity we feel with *illicit* touch, instead of ministering touch. We assume if we feel *felt* or if we have *felt* others, then it must be wrong. We suspect sinful motives in others or we fear our own sinful motives. That fear leads us to instate rules around touch, policies I've mentioned previously, like the Billy Graham Rule or the side hug or the quick, light, three-pat front hug between the same gender. Arm's length seems safest because we think it yields the least confusion. But it doesn't. As I've said before, it oftentimes can actually create more confusion, suspicion, fear, threat, and objectification.

The Stories We Carry

The people we meet inside the walls of our churches are walking through unspeakable suffering, trauma, pain, or confusion. Perhaps they were raised in abusive homes or were raped in college. Maybe they grew up under insufferable legalism or abject neglect. Their entire worldview has been shaped by the story they've lived and the wounds or scars they still bear. The same is true for us. I say unspeakable on purpose, because most of us don't even know how our histories have informed our todays, and even if we did, we don't know how to talk about it.

Each of us carries those stories with us into the foyers of church, beneath our church clothes and Christian clichés.

They rest on our shoulders as we slide into pews or plush chairs. They inform us as to whether we should reach out to touch, or withhold touch from one another. We're informed by the liturgies we repeat to ourselves when we're alone or the liturgies our culture tells us to believe. We feel unseen, unloved, or unknown. Every single person is fighting a battle within their heart, their mind, their body, or their soul. No one goes through life unscathed from the trauma of the living.

A few months after Nate and I married, I began bleeding one spectacular autumn afternoon. The blood came profusely and painfully and it wasn't long after it began that I realized: *I am miscarrying.*

Miscarriage is common. One in four pregnancies ends in it. We swallowed our grief and tried again. By the middle of December, I was pregnant again and we began to dream of names. But the first week of January ended with another intense miscarriage. Our mourning was deep and profound this time—coupled with some life circumstances that exacerbated our grief.

Over the next two years we would experience several more miscarriages—some we weren't even certain of until one doctor explained my condition more explicitly. I was unable to carry a baby past a certain number of weeks. Getting pregnant wasn't difficult—staying pregnant was.

We began to settle into a life of childlessness. Could God still bless our family if we remained childless? Were children—adopted, fostered, or medically induced through IVF—the only means of blessing for a Christian couple? Could there be what we came to call *a gift in this lack*? Was

God freeing up our home so we could parent children that our bodies did not create? Could the spare bedrooms in our house become home to young people who needed a place for a season? Could we settle into a life of repeated miscarriages or prevent future pregnancies, but either way remain faithful in our childlessness? The answer, for us, was yes.

But in June of 2018, I began to suspect again that I was pregnant, and further along than I had gotten in the past. One evening in late June, I began to bleed again. I began preparing my heart for another loss. But the bleeding didn't stop. It continued off and on for two weeks. I knew how to miscarry, but this didn't *feel* like a miscarriage; in fact, I felt normal. One night, though, I began to experience extreme abdominal pain. I have a high pain tolerance and an even higher distaste for drama, so I quickly disregarded Nate's suggestion that we go to the Emergency Room. After he saw my debilitating agony, he wisely overruled. In the ER, they immediately began drawing blood, putting me on high-powered drugs, firing questions at me faster than I could answer, and doing invasive internal ultrasounds. I mentioned my suspected miscarriage, but they told me the news was worse than I thought: the pregnancy was ectopic, the baby was attached to my fallopian tube, and unviable. I would die unless they removed the baby.

I am pro-life from womb to tomb, from conception to natural death. *Termination,* as they called it, didn't feel like an option to me. It was 3:00 am, but we immediately called a few elders from our church to seek counsel. I texted two of my closest friends, one a mother figure to me and the other a mother to eight. What should I do? To what lengths were we prepared to go to save my life? The baby wasn't viable, wouldn't survive, but I still couldn't reconcile the word *termination* with what was *still alive*. The moral crisis of it all was suffocating. We decided to remain in the hospital until they could tell us emphatically that I was about to die or the baby was dead. For the next five days, we, along with our small group and some pastors from our church, begged that God would miraculously move the baby from my tube into my uterus. We believed confidently He could—even if it was rare—and we asked that He would. Three days into our stay, one of our doctors shared a testimony of a time this seemed to have occurred for one of her patients and we slept that night in hope. As I drifted to sleep that night, surrounded by beeping machines and lights, I felt like this baby's name was Jubal: a worshipper of God in the presence of His people. I slept soundly that night.

Two days later, dizzy with morphine and the dropping of my already naturally low blood pressure, they wheeled me into an operating room and removed the baby, as well as irreparable parts of my reproductive system.

I bled for another four weeks.

We are, all of us, suffering from an issue of blood. For some that blood is real and red, signaling the loss of life in miscarriage, or the absence of life proven by the shed blood in our monthly cycles. For others that blood runs through our veins, passed down from our parents and grandparents and their parents and grandparents, flowing with the habits and harms of generational dysfunction. For others, our issue of blood is one of bloodline—the effects of things like systemic racism on us or through us. For yet others, it is a propensity toward anger or addiction or anxiety. The issue of blood for some is a skeptical mind or a naive one. For some, it's a disability or an inability to recover from a trauma inflicted by another or by ourselves. For some the issue is constant, and for others it is seasonal.

None of us is free from being cut by life, by sin, by the enemy, by ourselves. Yet, when we enter a room, we often forget the blood—the story—pulsing beneath the skin. We divorce bodies from their stories. Ragan Sutterfield, in his book, *This Is My Body*, said, "When we see people without recognizing that they have a story, we become pornographers. Pornography almost by definition lacks a story."[5] Sutterfield, provocative as he may be, is right. When we divorce a body from the story—the humanity and the life—that God has given it, it becomes a mere object to us. We can no more separate our blood from our bodies than we can separate our story from the bodies who have lived through it. We objectify our own bodies and the bodies of others if we dismiss the complexity of the story they have lived through and experienced.

When I finally made it back to church, nearly a month after our time in the hospital, I was still bleeding, carrying with me the evidence of a broken shalom, a fallen and sin-stricken world. I could not divorce myself from my story. None of us can.

---

[5] Ragan Sutterfield, *This Is My Body* (New York: Convergent Books, a division of Random House, 2015), 131.

In all my years of being in church, it was common to hear placid and stale counsel regarding touch. *Always* dos or *never* dos. But none of this takes into account the variety of stories the people of God carry with them—no two stories are alike, no two people are alike, therefore no two touches are alike in their giving or receiving. This makes it an infinitely complicated issue.

We don't need another how-to-do. We need an overhaul in how we think about humans and their stories, and how we interact with others as physical beings. We need discernment and Spirit-led love to know the caring ways to touch. We all carry with us an issue of blood. We are all cut by the Fall in different ways. And that means touch will come at us, and minister to us, and be given by us, in a myriad of ways as well. May God give us the discernment and the presence of mind to do all our stories justice in the way we touch.

Four Stories for All the Church

In Matthew 9 we see four stories of God's attentiveness toward a particular issue—and how Christ engages each with touch. Right after Jesus calls Matthew the tax-collector to follow Him, the Pharisees balked to His disciples: "Why does your teacher eat with tax-collectors and sinners?" Jesus responded, "It is not those who are well who need a doctor, but those who are sick. Go and learn what this means: I desire mercy and not sacrifice. For I didn't come to call the righteous, but sinners."[6]

---

[6] Matthew 9:11–13.

The whole message of Jesus was the expansive and expensive love of God for His people. Matthew spends the rest of chapter 9 proving Jesus' point.

First, Jesus is approached by a most religious Jew, a ruler of the synagogue, Jairus. The daughter of Jarius is dead, but he believes Jesus can heal by merely "laying a hand on her." Next, an unclean woman who has been bleeding for twelve years thinks to herself, *If I only touch His garment, I will be made well.* Then, Jesus makes His way to the daughter of Jairus, the dead little girl. Finally, two blind men beg for mercy and healing. Matthew is saying: all who call on the name of God can be saved, even the most religious, the most unclean, the youngest, and the blind—and he explicitly mentions the ministering touch of Jesus.

The four examples I use below should primarily be interpreted as the types of people Jesus came to save—the sick, the vulnerable, the blind, and so on. The big takeaway from these biblical passages is the lesson that those who know they are spiritually "sick" can be made well by Jesus, who ministers by touch in each case. Though these profiles primarily speak to the type of people who Jesus sought to rescue, meaning that they are usually the people we found outside the church, the truth is, we can see a lot of these types of people within the church too. After all, conversion—which includes coming to Christ with our poverty of spirit—is, of many things, simply a decision to *keep* coming to Him with our ailments and trials for the rest of our lives.

The Woman with the Issue of Blood: The Unclean

By Levitical law, the law by which God's people abided, the woman with the issue of blood in Matthew 9 would have been considered perpetually unclean. The Jewish term for her would have been *niddah*: the menstruating one. No one can menstruate (release an unfertilized egg) continuously over a period of twelve years, but the consistent presence of blood would have marked this woman as *untouchable*. Not only would she be considered untouchable by other humans, but anything she laid on, sat on, or touched would be considered unclean. Not only that, but anyone who touched anything that she touched would be considered unclean. She would be unable to have sex with a spouse, but even more so, she would be unable to experience a hug, a caress, a hand on the shoulder, or any physical contact whatsoever.

And she would know this.

She would be acutely aware of the stain her body left wherever she might go. The blood would be the least of her inconvenience, she—her *self*—was the chief inconvenience. Her body, every part of it and everything it touched, would be marked as unclean. Nowhere and nothing she touched for *twelve years* would be unscathed by her uncleanliness. She was her own worst enemy and she would have been viewed the same by anyone who knew her.

Countless doctors, countless monies, and countless tears had been spent on her condition and there was no answer, no fix, and no solace found for her. She was alone in her condition, alone in her life, and alone in her pain. And without a fix for her condition, she would continue on in physical isolation for the rest of her life. But, on a street nearby, a crowd was swarming, and Jesus was at its center.

The woman had heard about this Jesus who might heal and she thought, *Perhaps . . . if only . . . maybe if I merely touch His robe, I might be well.* She would have had to graze the sides and bump the shoulders of many in the group to get close to Jesus, something she'd be unable to do without hiding her identity from the crowd. Her faith most likely drew her to pull a heavy cloak over her body, hiding her face from anyone who might know her shame, and to dip her head down low, pushing her way through the heavy crowd to touch the robe of this Jesus. When she was within reach, her hand grazed the robe. Immediately she was made well, but the act was not without sacrifice.

"Who touched Me?" Jesus asked, perceiving His power had gone out from Him. His disciples responded in incredulity, "We're in this crowd and You're asking 'Who touched Me?'" In the Luke 8 telling of this story, it says that Jesus *kept looking.* And, it continues, the unclean woman fell on her face in fear before Him and told Him *the whole truth.* As Tim Keller in *Jesus the King* says, "He lost his power so she could gain it."[7] Jesus said to her, "Daughter, your faith has made you well; go in peace, and be healed of your disease." Keller goes on, "Why did Jesus insist that she go public [and answer His question, "Who touched me?"]? She needed the exposure. You see, she had a somewhat superstitious understanding of Jesus' power. She thought it was the touch that could heal her. She thought his power was manageable. And Jesus made

---

[7] Tim Keller, *Jesus the King* (New York: Penguin Books, 2016), 66.

her identify herself so he could say, 'Oh, no, it was faith that healed you.'"[8]

※ ※ ※

Into the doors of our churches will walk all kinds of people and most, if not all of us, will feel our uncleanliness. We will feel the stain of our sin, the division between us and God, the fracture between us and other people. We might not even have words for sin or conviction, but we know the brokenness of being other than, different, outcast, and unloved. Even the most physically beautiful or athletic, the most put together or intelligent, will still feel at their core unworthy, unseen, unloved, or overlooked. Every human suffers from an issue of blood—not just the bloodline of our own story, but the bloodline of all humanity that began at the Fall: sin. And, like the woman in the gospel's narrative, we shroud ourselves in whatever will cover our blemishes and hide our true selves. We know if people really knew who we were, they would want nothing to do with us.

We collect faith and collect ourselves and think, *Perhaps today, I will meet Jesus, I will be touched by Him or touch Him. Perhaps today He will heal my systemic issues, my historical habits, my body's brokenness, my issue of blood.*

And then we walk through the doors of the church. Perhaps we walk through as newcomers or seasoned congregants or church staff or even a pastor. We walk in, cloaked in

---

[8] Ibid., 70.

whatever will cover the week's suffering and brokenness, and we beg to meet Jesus.

Our Savior, in the midst of the swarming crowd, in the midst of dedicated disciples, feels our presence, our touch. He senses it so strongly that He stops, asks, and *keeps looking* for us. Jesus taught about being a good shepherd who leaves the ninety-nine for the one and, here He is, in a sea of people, stopping for the one. He does that for us too—those with the perpetual issues of blood, who take every shred of faith we have and bring it with us to His church in hopes that we might meet Him.

And He knows it, He *feels* His power going out to us, and He keeps looking for us. And when He finds us, it is only then that we can freely tell Him our whole story. We forget the cloak, the swarming crowd, the past twelve years, the belief that it's His touch that will make us well. We meet Him and tell Him everything. "Go in peace," He says, "Your faith has made you well."

Within the church we can be tempted to declare certain people touchable and others untouchable. We can grow confused ourselves about when and how it's appropriate to touch them, but in this narrative Jesus allows Himself to be touched, allows the power to go out of Him. He makes Himself vulnerable for the sake of the vulnerable. He makes Himself touchable, proximal, within reach of our needy hands.

I love that in this passage, Jesus doesn't touch the unclean woman; she touches Him. She is the marginalized one, the one considered unclean. The gospel narrative shows us her initiating faith and initiating action. She touches Jesus, not the other way around.

What if, instead of Christians making decisions about how to touch newcomers and attendees, we allowed them to carry their faith and brokenness *in tandem* with them and *to decide themselves* how to touch *us* as conduits of Christ? What if leaders carried authority and vulnerability in tension with one another—walking in the strength and knowledge that we are God's and on His mission, and could, therefore, allow ourselves to be made vulnerable, like Jesus did, for the sake of those who have only known the kind of vulnerability that leads to exploitation in their life and bloodline? What if, like Him, we could make ourselves approachable regarding touch within the church, instead of drawing lines every which way in order to preserve the ideas people have about us?[9]

---

[9] Most of my thoughts on vulnerability and strength have been formed by Andy Crouch's book, *Strong and Weak*, and in particular, his quadrant on authority and vulnerability. He illustrates a four-square with arrows forming the cross-section. The vertical arrow is "Authority" and the horizontal is "Vulnerability." Andy says that authority without vulnerability is exploitation, vulnerability without authority is suffering, a void of both vulnerability *and* authority leads to withdrawing, and authority *with* vulnerability leads to flourishing. This has been a helpful rubric for me to think through as I write because so many of the abuses of touch are explained in the exploitive, suffering, or withdrawn quadrant, and the healthy expressions of it exist where both parties have both authority *and* vulnerability in tandem. In the case of the woman with the issue of blood, she was the vulnerable one who walked in a semblance of authority, and reached out to touch Jesus, and therefore flourished. While we cannot offer healing to everyone (only Jesus is Healer), we can posture ourselves like Jesus in this: going about our Father's business in the authority He's given us and yet allowing ourselves to be made vulnerable (touchable)

God in flesh allowed Himself to be made vulnerable so the broken might be healed. We cannot fully heal people by touching them, but we recognize their humanity, their story, their issue of blood, by allowing ourselves to be touched by them. Like Jesus, we should simply make ourselves within reach, available to however God might use us in His healing narrative.

The Daughter Who Was Dead: The Child

The story of the unclean woman takes place in the midst of the crowd around Jesus—a crowd that was following Him on His way to heal the daughter of a local ruler. The child's father had come to Jesus and pled with Him, saying she was "at the point of death."[10] He continued, "Come and lay your hands on her, so that she maybe be made well and live." Jesus, with the crowd on His heels, made His way to the ruler's house, healing the unclean woman along the way.

When Jesus and the crowd arrived at the home, some came out and said to the ruler, "It's too late, your daughter is dead. Don't trouble the Teacher any more." Jesus admonished them saying, "Do not fear, only believe." He walked in the home where the mourners were weeping and wailing loudly. Moments later, their grief is waylaid by laughter at Jesus when He insists the little girl is merely sleeping. He sends them outside and went to where the little one was lying. He took

---

by others. Both the ministry of Jesus and the woman flourished in this narrative because they both were exercising authority and vulnerability.
[10] Mark 5:23 (ESV).

her hand and said, "Talitha cumi," which means, "Little girl, I say to you, arise." And the girl stood up and began walking.

❁ ❁ ❁

I belong to a large church in the Dallas-Fort Worth metroplex. Ten years ago our church body was full of singles and young married couples, but in the last few years, there has been an explosion of little ones. As I write this we've been in a season of trying to discern what changes to make with our present building to accommodate all the new babies or if perhaps we need a new one.

As we've been adding these little ones to our congregation, story after story has dominated the news, reporting that church members or church leaders have abused others, sometimes even children. Not wanting to be naive to the possibility or probability of abuse taking place within our local church, our leaders and volunteers have sought wisdom and training to spot abuse, neglect, or inappropriate behavior across the board. By God's grace, this has led to more awareness and safety within our body, while simultaneously bringing past issues to light that require the intervention of civil authorities. We mourn what has been broken and give thanks to God for bringing it to light. And we also continue to desire wisdom, not naiveté, about the commonness of abuse.

In many (though not all) of these cases coming to light in churches across the country and world, the perpetrator strangely assumed that the young victim was much more mature than he or she actually was, and also assumed that their touch would somehow be welcomed, wanted, or even fully understood. In many cases, they claim they thought it was consensual. They wrongly conferred the emotions, decision-making, and cognitive ability of an adult to a child. They did not call a child a child. They touched a child sinfully, not acknowledging who they actually were, but instead making them into whatever they wanted them to be. They used children for sinful pleasure, sinful gain, sinful power grabbing, and sinful abuse.

As we navigate the issue of child abuse within the church, we have to be incredibly vigilant to eradicate any sinful forms of touch while also being careful not to neglect children. After all, we should seek to engage children the way Christ did. Christ did draw children near to Him, but in every situation in Scripture in which He did, He *always* names them as children. He declares to those around Him: this is a child. These are children. This is a little girl. This is a little boy. To the disciples fussing about the little children clamoring to be around Jesus, He says, "Let the little children come to me."[11] To the disciples arguing about who would be the greatest in the kingdom, Jesus draws a little boy to Him and said they must "become like little children."[12] In this narrative, He calls the little girl what she is before reaching His hand out to her.

I believe in recent years the American church has been given a great opportunity to repent for the ways in which

---

[11] Mark 10:14.

[12] Direct quote of Christ from Matthew version of this story (Matt. 18:3). Luke's version of this moment reveals the child as a boy (Luke 9:47–48).

we have treated little ones in the past. The light is blinding in some ways as we shine it on what has been dark—many will lose their jobs, position, or reputations in the process. And though there have been mistakes, oversights, or willful ignorance in the process or false accusations raised, we have the opportunity to remember the children and remind them and others who they are: vulnerable, little, immature, not the adult they will someday be. Knowing this, we must touch them with understanding, care, and respect for who they are, just as Jesus did.

Immediately after Jesus places His hand on the little one (something her father was not only present for and permitted, but personally requested), she was raised to life. In the Luke 8 narrative, after the little girl resurrects, Jesus directed the witnesses to give her something to eat. I love this. Jesus is again reminding those around her that she needs to be cared for, not expected to care for others. He is reminding them she is vulnerable and requires help, nourishment, and protection.

When my youngest sibling was born, nearly three months early, he was in an incubator for weeks and we measured every single gram he gained. The thing I remember most about that time was how translucent his skin was. It was as though he'd gotten very badly sunburned, his skin was red and papery, thin and fragile. Though he should have still been safe and growing inside my mother's womb, he was instead subject to the lights and prods and pricks of being born too soon. We were barely allowed to touch him. His skin could hardly handle contact and his body was too vulnerable to germs. I lamented that loss of touch, thinking surely if we could just hold him close he would grow faster. But doctors, in their wisdom, kept our hands away from him until the proper time.

When we touch a child, we must remember we are touching a vulnerable thing, one who is not what they will be, and some touch is not for their good. Their reality is not the same as an adult's reality and we must engage them with touch as *they* are, not just as we are. As Dietrich Bonhoeffer says, "To bear the burden of the other person means involvement with the created reality of the other, to accept and affirm it, and, in bearing with it, to break through to the point where we take joy in it."[13] We see this kind of joy in Jesus when the disciples tried to hold the children back from Him. Again, Jesus named them as children before laying His hands on them, "'Leave the children alone, and don't try to keep them from coming to me, because the kingdom of heaven belongs to such as these.' After placing his hands on them, he went on from there."[14] This is the sort of joy with which the touching of children should be expressed—not the secretive, furtive attempts to exploit *or* the panicked, rigid attempts to control. By calling children what they are and bearing their burdens, we can touch them as they really are, not as we wish they were. We exhibit this when we take a knee when speaking to a child, bringing our adult face to their level, instead of requiring them to simply look up to us. We meet them at their reality (their vulnerability) instead of forcing them to come to ours.

---

[13] Dietrich Bonhoeffer, *Life Together* (New York: Harper & Row Publishers, Inc., Harper Collins, 1954), 101.
[14] Matthew 19:14–15 (ESV).

In this story of healing the daughter of Jarius, Jesus meets the little girl as she is, declares what she is, offers her healing and healthy touch, and releases her *whole,* back into the care of her parents to get nourishment to keep growing and maturing into the adult she will someday be. So we should do as we interact with children—whether that be the way we teach them on Sunday mornings, babysit them on the weekends, or disciple them in our own homes.

The Two Blind Men: The Skeptics

As Jesus went on, Matthew tells us, two blind men passed Him, crying out, "Have mercy on us, Son of David." Jesus asked, "Do you believe that I am able to do this?" And they responded, "Yes, Lord." Jesus touched their eyes and said, "According to your faith be it done to you."[15]

❈ ❈ ❈

There's a third group of people in our churches: the blind.

I opened this chapter with recollections about my history in church, but what I didn't say is that my years in a denomination that highly valued how one felt about God ended with me in a dark season of doubt. In the face of overwhelming sadness, loss, grief, and more, I could not bring my emotions into submission under the Word of God on my own. The response to my sadness was, "Why can't you just believe God is good?" The response to my doubt was, "Pray more.

---

[15] Matthew 9:27–29.

Memorize more Scripture. Worship God more. Practice the gifts of the Spirit more." The response to my grief was, "Mourning lasts for the night but joy comes in the morning—and look! It's morning!" All around my life was loss in the form of death, divorce, poverty, court orders, and more. I was in a season of severe personal trauma with no rubric for how to claw out except to "Speak in tongues more often," and I didn't speak in tongues at all. I didn't know what truth was but I knew it couldn't be to just simply *do more.*

Looking back, what I now know about that season is that I was blind to God's faithfulness, goodness, and especially His sovereignty, and there was nothing I could do to open my own eyes. I wasn't actually a Christian yet. I may have rubbed shoulders with some found people, and even assumed I was among them, but the truth was I was lost, and I couldn't see. I needed Jesus. I needed Him to "Open my eyes so that I may contemplate wondrous things from [His] instruction" (Ps. 119:18). Until He opened my eyes, it wouldn't matter what I did—I would still be blind.

God, in His great mercy, led me to the end of myself one night after a few years of denying my doubt in Him, His goodness, and finally His existence. I was able to admit to Him (the irony is not lost on me in speaking to One I didn't think existed), "I don't believe You exist, and if You do exist, I don't believe You're good, and if You are good, I don't believe You're good to me, and I won't serve a god like that anymore." I rose from my snot-soaked carpet where I'd been laying, and felt a freedom unlike any I've ever felt before. I was the opposite of a Christian at this point, but my honesty before God was one major thing that led to my eventual salvation. I had to go through the confession of where I really was with God before I could get to where I'd eventually end up.

A few years after this experience, after I'd come to a saving knowledge of Christ and believed the gospel, I read a passage in Martyn Lloyd-Jones's book, *Spiritual Depression*, where he wrote of Jesus curing another blind man but with two separate touches to his eyes. With the first, the blind man could see, but not well. Upon the second touch of Jesus, the man could see clearly.[16] Lloyd-Jones says:

> What is the cure for [spiritual depression]? . . . [F]irst: *above everything else avoid making premature claim that your blindness is cured.* It must have been a great temptation to this man to do that. Here is a man who has been blind. Our Lord puts spittle upon his eyes and says to him: "Do you see?" The man says: "I see." What a temptation it must have been to him to take to his heels and announce to the whole world: "I can see!'" The man, in a sense, could see, but so far his sight was incomplete and imperfect, and it was most vital that he should not testify before he had seen clearly.[17]

Lloyd-Jones continues with the opposite mistake though:

---

[16] Mark 8:22–26.

[17] Martyn Lloyd-Jones, *Spiritual Depression* (Grand Rapids: Wm. B. Eerdmans Publishing Co., 1965), 46–47.

The temptation to the first is to run and to proclaim that they can see, before they see clearly; but the temptation to the second is to feel absolutely hopeless and to say: "There is no point in going on. You have put spittle on my eyes and you have touched me. In a sense I see, but I am simply seeing men as if they were trees walking." . . .

What then is the cure? What is the right way? *It is to be honest and to answer our Lord's question truthfully and honest.* That is the whole secret of this matter. He turned to this man and asked: "Do you see [anything]?" And the man said, absolutely honestly: "I *do* see, but I am seeing men as if they were trees walking." What saved this man was his absolutely honesty.

Now the question is, where do we stand? . . . What exactly do we see? Have we got things clearly? . . . Do we know God? Do we know Jesus Christ? Not only as our Saviour but do we know Him? . . . Let us be honest; let us face the questions, let us face them with absolute honesty.[18]

Though I don't think it was the man's honesty that healed him (*Jesus* healed him), I agree with Lloyd-Jones that our honesty about our state plays a major part in our experience

---

[18] Ibid.

of Jesus, whether that be the moment of our conversion or difficult moments along the path of our Christian journey. These two blind men whom Jesus came across in Matthew 9 were quickly honest about their state: they knew they needed mercy and they believed Jesus could extend it. Jesus could— and He chose to extend it through His touch.

When skeptics walk through the doors of our churches and we hold them at a physical distance until they *see* clearly, we do not model the body of Jesus, who reached out and touched the ones who acted in faith by simply showing up. There was no guarantee Jesus would see or heal the blind men in Matthew 9, but they showed up, blindness and all. There's a reason I say God's best mercy to me began the night I denied Him on the floor of my rented home. It is because that was the night I began to be honest about who, what, and where I was before Him. I couldn't touch Him on my own, and He couldn't touch me in a way I'd feel, until I was honest about my blindness.

Just as everyone has some metaphorical (or physical) issue of blood, every person is a blind skeptic in some way. Perhaps we doubt God's existence or His goodness toward us. Perhaps we doubt His plan will work for us. Maybe we doubt His love for us or His faithfulness. We are all just a little bit blind, and we need the touch of Jesus to help us see. So how does Jesus remove the blinders in today's time, helping us see the truth when we are wallowing in lies, or fear, or doubt? How does Jesus touch our eyes now that He's no longer walking the earth? Through the touches of His body—our spiritual brothers and sisters and fathers and mothers in the church.

Their pure and healthy touch can be a conduit for the touch of Christ to be made evident in our lives. Jesus is still moving throughout the earth, ministering and touching those who need His care, and He does so through His people. If we'd let Him.

During the same season I wrestled with deep doubt, an unbeliever with no church background frequently visited the house in which I lived with a few other girls. I remember him remarking one night as we sat around talking philosophy, art, and other ideas, that he'd never been hugged as well as I hugged him. I glanced up sharply, wondering if he was making a sexual innuendo or a joke, but he had tears in his eyes as he looked across the room at me. "There's something healing in your touch," he said.

There wasn't total healing in my touch the same way that Jesus can offer healing touch, of course, but in a certain sense, there was a type of healing in my hug that offered a glimpse of what human touch should do for others. Even in my season of unbelief and doubt, the Spirit was willing and working in me to bring about eventual faith and, in the meantime, an expression of healing. Two doubters in different stages of belief and unbelief, met, hugged, and mended just a little bit more of what felt hopelessly broken in the world. As we sat there, two spiritually blind people, God was giving us both a dimly lit picture of what pure and restorative interaction could look like. We may not have been able to see God clearly in that moment, but through one good experience of touch we could make out trees, blurry as they were, and that was a step forward.

Everyone needs touch, but perhaps the skeptics need it most of all.

Jarius the Synagogue Ruler: The Legalist

In every church we will find the bleeding, the vulnerable, and the skeptic to some degree, but we are surrounded by the last category—the legalist. I said in the beginning of this chapter that legalism has in many ways formed the basis for how, when, and who we touch within the church. We add to the Word of God instead of letting it lead us. We draw tighter boundaries and clearer distinctions and think of people primarily as bodies instead of humans with stories, vulnerabilities, and doubts. This chapter in many ways is written *to* the legalists among us. But even a legalist needs touch.

In Matthew 9:18, we're simply told a "ruler" came in and begged Jesus to heal his dead daughter, but in Luke 8, we're given more context about who this ruler was. His name was Jarius, and he was a ruler in the synagogue—an official who was in charge of arranging synagogue services, which included organizing the flow of events and sometimes teaching in the service. It is very likely that this man was a Pharisee. This means he'd be a letter-of-the-extended-law legalist who would have known more acutely than anyone that touching a dead body meant becoming unclean. His request? "Come and lay your hand on her and she will live." A word of healing wouldn't be enough for this desperate father; he wanted the touch of Jesus upon his daughter, the touch that would make Jesus unclean. In other words, he was willing to put his legalism aside to see Jesus move, to see someone dead come alive.

※ ※ ※

As long as Christians shape their lives and interactions with others, and curate how, who, when, and what they'll touch with their physical hands, according to legalistic laws and codes of conduct, we are like the other Pharisees who most certainly would have judged Jarius's plea to Jesus just as they judged the actions of Jesus Himself. But if we humble ourselves and kneel before the Healer, begging for His touch on our own lives, bodies, families, and homes, submitting to the fact that we are earthly beings with earthly deaths and earthly laments, we will see God. If we are willing to put our one-size-fits-all rules about touch to the side, we might just see Jesus move. Through both our message of the gospel and our ministering touch that embodies it, we might just see God raise the spiritually dead to life.

Choosing to Be a Church of Touch

God loves it when we're honest about our own inability to heal ourselves and others, because truth be told, though we can certainly minister with our touch in *meaningful* ways, only He can touch a broken vessel in a *miraculous* way. Only He can heal issues of blood from generations past, only He can touch that which is too vulnerable and tender to touch, only He can heal our blindness through honesty, and only He can heal our legalism through the gift of humility.

But here's the thing: He uses His people on earth as an expression of His healing. He uses our hands and feet and bodies and hugs. He uses a hand on the shoulder of a brother at church, a squeeze that says, "I'm here, and I see you." He uses the shoulders of strangers touching in a row in a sanctuary to say, "You are not alone." He uses hands laid on toddlers and babies and little ones in prayer to say, "You are so small now, but God is with you." He uses the touch of unclean people to remind us of how unclean we all would be without the robe of His grace. He uses the touch of pastors to show how our Good Shepherd leads us *by His own hand* (Pss. 73:23–24; 95:7; 139:10; Isa. 41:10). He uses all of our good and godly touch to reveal just how wide His mercy is and how good His love is.

Ragan Sutterfield says it well:

> The church should be a place where we remember our bodies and learn the communion of touch. It is in the church that we eat and taste the earthbound flesh of Christ: the body and the blood of communion . . . we baptize the body in water, immersing the new believers by lowering them into the baptismal pool. . . . "Greet one another with a holy kiss" says Paul. . . . [There is] the washing of feet, an experience both tender and uncomfortable. I mourn for those who cannot let their bodies come forward to be served and to serve

the body as Christ served the bodies of his followers.[19]

Your body is a temple, yes, but a temple is not the thing to be worshipped. Your body is a dwelling place for the Spirit of God, who gives you the ability to worship God and live rightly among His people and the world. And, as Sutterfield points out, part of living rightly means using our temples—our bodies—to offer healing touches to the church body. So, among many things we do as we gather weekly for worship, all believers should bring both our souls *and* our bodies forward to "be served and to serve," and then go out into all the world and do the same for all those who don't know Christ, whether they be the unclean, the child, the skeptic, or the legalist. After all, you and I may be the only Jesus they ever see or touch.

---

[19] Ragan Sutterfield, *This Is My Body* (New York: Convergent Books, a division of Random House, 2015), 114.

CHAPTER FOUR

Touch of Self

If any thing is sacred the human body is sacred.[1]
—Walt Whitman

I have spent my whole life in Sunday school, but it wasn't until I was on the cusp of thirty that I truly heard the words, "In the beginning." It was then that the starting point—or *person*, rather—of the full gospel was unveiled to me.

There were no flannel boards or animated vegetables singing this elementary line from Genesis 1, just one woman behind a podium at my new church. She spent a whole hour teaching from this one sentence, "In the beginning, God created."[2] The genesis of my life in Christ was birthed that

---

[1] Walt Whitman, "I Sing the Body Electric," *The Complete Poems of Walt Whitman* (Hertfordshire: Wordsworth Editions Limited, 1995), 76.
[2] Genesis 1:1.

night when I saw, for the first time, what I had known deep-down as true, but never had words for until now. I saw God's existence as wholly non-contingent upon my own. He was always there, from the beginning, even when I wasn't. In the beginning, *God*. Full stop. Before He created anything, He was God, and He always had been. The only thing that was there in the beginning was God. Not us. Not me. Not the world. Not anything but God. In that moment I knew God to be truly holy.

It's impossible to fully understand the nature of God from a limited, fallen point of view. We are humans with histories and futures and, while we might have no trouble seeing God as over and above and around us, it is difficult to see His actions as wholly independent from us. He was before we were. He is before we are. And He will always be just as He is. Unchangeable, yesterday, today, and forever (Heb. 1:12; 13:8; Rev. 1:8).

It was this holy God that John pointed his readers toward with the opening words of his gospel. "In the beginning," he begins, echoing Genesis 1:1, "was the Word."[3]

John's first readers would have known right away the significance of this phrase. John was repeating ideas they had heard thousands of times in their life—in particular, the opening line of their Torah. "He's talking about God," they would have whispered to one another as they heard John's gospel read aloud, "and the Word was with God, and the Word was God. He was with God in the beginning. All things were created through him, and apart from him not

---

[3] John 1:1.

one thing was created that has been created. In him was life, and that life was the light of men. That light shines in the darkness, and yet the darkness did not overcome it."[4] Just reading those words gives me chills: this is our God. Before all things, and magnificently ethereal to our earthly eyes.

He is wholly apart from us.

He is wholly *apart* from us.

He can be worshipped, but can He be known?

As John goes on in verses 6–14, John's answer is yes. He says that instead of remaining altogether apart from us, God came into the world to be with us, and not as a concept or idea, but a tangible being. And then in verse 14, John gives it to us straight: "The Word became flesh and dwelt among us. We observed his glory, the glory as the one and only Son from the Father, full of grace and truth."[5]

How can a transcendent, holy God be known? By putting on flesh. By becoming one of His own.

Verse 14 of the first chapter of John is the verse upon which our faith takes a new shape. With these words God no longer feels too grand to be known, too separate to be loved, too tidy to get dirty, too distant to be touched. He is no longer only a far-off Creator, invisible to His creation. He came near by coming down here to earth. In Christ, He became God with us. *Emmanuel.*

Every one of the four Gospels that make up the beginning of the New Testament confirm that God dwelt among His creation as flesh, a human being, pulsing with the

---

[4] John 1:1–5.
[5] John 1:14.

lifeblood of mankind. That means He shares in the human experience. He was born from the womb of a woman, covered in afterbirth and squalling for His mother's breasts. He likely learned to walk holding on to the rough stonemason hands of His earthly father. He probably fell and scraped His knee, running for it to be kissed and cleaned and bandaged by His mother. He slept fitfully. He slept deeply. He had dreams. He likely woke His parents too early when He was small and slept in too late when He got older. He washed mud from His feet and food from His hands. He caught colds and knew temptation (Heb. 4:15). He had to learn the Jewish Scriptures as a child and grew up like any other person in His village. He got tired and weary after long days, and had to learn obedience (John 4:6; Heb. 5:8). As we see in some passages, He was the wisest guy in the room, infuriating some and astounding others. God, in Christ, came and was *knowable.*

With the coming of Jesus to earth, God's characteristics were expressed concretely in the body of Jesus. It was no longer abstract goodness, faithfulness, and creator, but concrete expressions of kindness, gentleness, justice, and self-control. He was perfect and He was flesh. He touched and was touched. He touched kindly and was touched unkindly. He touched to heal the sick and was touched by those looking to steal His dignity. He touched to remind His people that He was *here* and *with them,* and was touched to be reminded that His life was not His own. Though He could have come whenever and wherever in time and in the universe, He lived in a particular place at a particular time with a particular people. *Hier zu sein ist so viel,* the poet Rilke wrote. "To be here is so immense."[6] For Christ it truly was. The incarnation was the most immense action of all time for all men.

❉ ❉ ❉

It matters that God came as a human in the flesh, without sin, yet tempted in every way by it.[7] It means we not only have a God we can know, but who also truly knows what it's like to be us. Without God in flesh, our confidence would wobble even more than it already does in those moments of potent temptation. We have a great high priest who is better than a mere mediator, but who is still a mediator who *has known temptation*, and who, even better, we *know* because He's been there before too.

God, in flesh, the Word, Jesus Christ, came and dwelt with a particular people in a particular place, and that reality still matters to us in these "appointed times and the boundaries of where [we] live" (Acts 17:26). The fullness of God, the Word, came as Jesus Christ in the fullness of embodied humanity and that means we have reason to fully experience our embodied humanity as well. The trouble is, we don't always get that right.

---

[6] Rainer Maria Rilke, Unknown, quoted in *To Bless the Space Between Us*, John O'Donohue (New York: Doubleday, 1998), 186.
[7] Hebrews 4:15.

Your Body Matters to God

A few years ago, amidst experiencing several traumatic events in a row (including several miscarriages, moving cross-country three times in less than two years, and my husband's unemployment), I came home from work one day to my home cordoned off by caution tape. A felon had been killed behind my home by SWAT officers. A few short weeks later I became a witness to another violent crime, the shooting of a police officer at close range. Suffice it to say, it became a rough year for me when it came to taking care of my body. There were days I was afraid to leave the house or drive in my car alone. I found myself thirty pounds heavier, eating healthy sporadically, exercising never, feeling anxious almost constantly, and showering every few days. I did not have the energy to deal with my flesh. I knew something was wrong and had been for a while, but I felt alone in my struggle. Some days it was all I could do to wake up, make coffee, walk our dog, and work from home a few hours before the anxiety got unbearable.

Overwhelmed by my fears and anxieties, I'd run a hot bath in the ancient bathtub of our 1890s home outside Washington, D.C. I would pour in some Epsom salts, sink into the water, and tell myself to breathe. Sometimes I'd bring a book along. This is where I read Kathleen Norris's *The Quotidan Mysteries* and *Acedia and Me*, and where I reread Barbara Kingsolver's *Animal, Vegetable, Miracle*, and where I recited poems from Madeleine L'Engle and Wendell Berry. I would get out, get dry, and apply homemade balm over my shoulders, my shins, and my cuticles. I would brush my hair, running conditioner through its unruly strands. Then I would cover my eyes, nose, cheeks, temples, and neck with moisturizer, working in deep circles until it was all fully absorbed and my skin felt replenished. Finally, I would put on fresh clothing and make dinner.

Nothing about my insides (or outsides) changed in that season (or the season after), but for one hour, my soul felt at peace. In the furiously swirling and changing world, where every single thing felt out of my control, something as simple as touching my own face, hands, and hair reminded me that I was mere flesh and blood, not a superhuman. I could just breathe. My sense of safety and autonomy had been stolen from me and those few moments in the bath gave it back to me as I pondered the God who came in flesh like mine and knew its limitations.

I still don't have the energy most days to deal with myself, but a shift began to happen this past summer. I know that in order for some of these bad habits to change, I cannot just ignore them, I have to care about them. I have to care about my body; I have to care about my *self.*

The idea of "self-care"—especially through self-touch, may be a ubiquitous topic in our culture, but isn't popular in some circles. In a conversation with a friend a few months ago, a fellow believer, I mentioned the words "self-care" and she scoffed. "Oh goodness," she said, "Everyone is talking about self-care these days. It's become an idol where everyone is looking for the latest mask or best skin-care routine or getting monthly massages or manicures. It's so selfish. God will take care of our bodies. We shouldn't place such a high premium on our bodies and the care of them. We're going to get new ones anyway, and we'll have wasted all the time we could be building the kingdom by getting pedicures and doing face masks." She sneered the last part and I felt embarrassed. It was precisely the act of caring for myself, my *self,* my embodied self, that was teaching me about the limitations of my body and its need to submit to care. My neglect of it had ramped up all kinds of physical issues.

As I considered the importance of caring for my self, I noticed that a whole new part of Scripture was being opened up to me. I could see in the Bible how part of the kingdom work—the part my friend sneered at—was happening when Jesus healed people's physical bodies. The kingdom of heaven was coming to earth, and it was changing bodies, not just in eternity, but on earth too. Yes, those healings and miracles were signposts that pointed to spiritual realities of God's ability to rescue and regenerate and restore, but the fact still remains that *Jesus cared for people's bodies.* On top of the miraculous ways He healed people, He also did the subtle things. He lifted chins, He touched faces, He wiped tears, He washed feet. And when it comes to His own body, Jesus wasn't off getting pedicures or going to spa weekends, but He also did not neglect His own physical body. He took a rest when He was tired. He pulled away when He needed to. He slept. He ate. He drank. He walked. He took care of His incarnated body, and so should we.

I also noticed that Paul, who is known for calling out the sinful ways in which God's people use their bodies, also saw the good in our instinct to seek comfort for our bodies, as we see in his letter to the church at Ephesus. Talking about how to care for households, Paul says, "Husbands should love their wives as their own bodies. He who loves his wife, loves himself. For no one ever hated his own flesh, but nourishes and cherishes it, just as Christ does the church because we are members of his body."[8] In this passage on how to care for a wife, Paul presupposes that every man attempting to care for his wife, to nourish and cherish her body, is already familiar with the nourishment and care of his *own* body. He doesn't shame the man for knowing how to nourish and cherish his own body. He doesn't tell him to neglect the nourishment and cherishing of his own body. He doesn't even say to nourish and cherish her body *more* than he does his own. He says, "Just as you do for your own body, do for hers." Paul isn't simply giving the husband permission to care for his own body, he is saying it is massively important. The good and natural impulse to take care of one's body is actually the grounding for his argument. If the husband were to neglect the care and nourishment of his own body, he would be unable to appropriately nourish and cherish the body of his spouse—or anyone else. Like the oxygen mask in the airplane, we put it on ourselves before we're any good to anyone else.

Most of us don't like this because it sounds selfish or it doesn't sound Christlike, but it isn't selfish. Christ's ultimate goal was to honor the body he had by submitting to its intended purpose: to lay it down for the lives of God's children. Jesus Himself cared for His own earthly body when it required the things all bodies require—this is why we see

---

[8] Ephesians 5:28–30 (esv).

Him eating, drinking, sleeping, stopping to rest at a well, and so on. To be like Jesus, we must submit to the reality that we have physical limitations and requirements for our bodies to function and carry out the vocation and purposes God has intended.

In addition to reading the Bible and seeing these things, I was also reading up on the relationship between the body, the soul, the mind, and the heart. Did you know that our bodies remember and change when we've gone through trauma? My doctors were saying to me—for the first time!—*go easy on yourself, be gentle, you've gone through a lot.* This whole new world of caring for myself not only as a temple of the Spirit, but an in-flesh *embodied* human, was being opened to me. And, simultaneously, Christian culture was not a welcome place for the words "self-care" or "self-touch"—the only response I got from them was someone scoffing in response.

This war against all things physical is no stranger in Christian thought. Paul warned the Colossians about the uprising of a new brand of so-called Christians who argued the body was of no account and we ought not concern ourselves with it, or any physical pleasure for that matter. It's a Greek idea starting with Plato—an ancient heresy, really—that we have come to call dualism. Ancient people were elevating religiousness or spirituality above the very real human body in which all people existed. The body, according to a dualist, is inherently evil, something your soul is imprisoned by. And the highest form of spirituality was to escape your body and achieve being only spirit. In short, physical was bad and spiritual was good.

Paul didn't take this idea lightly. He knew that God created us as holistic beings—mind, body, and spirit together as one. He knew that God created the physical world and that God called it *good*. It wasn't evil. He told the Colossians they were in danger of being taken "captive through philosophy and empty deceit based on human tradition, based on the elements of the world, rather than Christ."[9]

To counter this empty gospel and remind his readers (and us) of the truth, Paul continued on, saying,

> For the entire fullness of God's nature dwells bodily in Christ, and you have been filled by him, who is the head over every ruler and authority. You were also circumcised in him with a circumcision not done with hands, by putting off the body of flesh, in the circumcision of Christ, when you were buried with him in baptism, in which you were also raised with him through faith in the working of God, who raised him from the dead. And when you were dead in trespasses and in the uncircumcision of your flesh, he made you alive with him and forgave us all our trespasses. He erased the certificate of debt, with its obligations, that was against us and opposed to us, and has taken it away by nailing it to the cross. He disarmed the rulers and

---

[9] Colossians 2:8.

authorities and disgraced them publicly; he triumphed over them in him.

Therefore, don't let anyone judge you in regard to food and drink or in the matter of a festival or a new moon or a Sabbath day. These are a shadow of what was to come; the substance is Christ. Let no one condemn you by delighting in ascetic practices and the worship of angels, claiming access to a visionary realm. Such people are inflated by empty notions of their unspiritual mind. He doesn't hold on to the head, from whom the whole body, nourished and held together by its ligaments and tendons, grows with growth from God.[10]

Throughout his explanation, it's easy to notice that Paul uses words that describe the physical and the tangible: *body, hands, flesh, circumcision, buried, baptism, raised, dead, alive, head, nourished, knit, joints, ligaments*, and *growth*. Paul is saying instead of concerning ourselves *less* with the body, we should concern ourselves *more* with it in its *proper* way. He is saying: the body matters and that's why the "fullness of deity" came and "dwelt bodily" with us. If only ethereal and spiritual things mattered, Jesus would not have had to come. He would not have come. Why would it matter for Him to come?

I found a kindred Christian spirit, not a scoffer, in Wendell Berry as well. In his essay, "The Body and the

---

[10] Colossians 2:9–19.

Earth," he writes: "You cannot devalue the body and value the soul—or value anything else." Berry didn't sneer at self-care, he knew it had much bigger implications. "Contempt for the body is invariably manifested in contempt for other bodies—the bodies of slaves, laborers, women, animals, plants, the earth itself. Relationships with all other creatures become competitive and exploitive rather than collaborative and convivial. . . . The body is degraded and saddened by being set in conflict against Creation itself, of which all bodies are members, therefore members of each other. The body is thus sent to war against itself."[11]

We, Christians especially, can sometimes value the soul at expense of the body because we know someday these current bodies will pass away (though we often forget that they will be raised and glorified in the resurrection). But even if our current bodies as we know them won't last, God cares about the bodies we inhabit in the here and now. Our entire faith hinges on the fact that Jesus came in a body and died in a body and was raised in a body. God must care deeply about our bodies. And for all C. S. Lewis's head-scratching thoughts on heaven and hell, he had some excellent thoughts on matter: "There is no good trying to be more spiritual than God. God never meant man to be a purely spiritual creature. That is why He uses material things like bread and wine to put the new life into us. We may think this rather crude and unspiritual. God does not: He invented eating. *He likes*

---

[11] Wendell Berry, "The Body and the Earth," *Art of the Commonplace* (Emeryville, CA: Shoemaker & Hoard, 2002), 101.

matter. He invented it."[12] If our bodies matter to God, they should matter to us. And they should matter to us as they *are*, not only how they will someday be.

Your Body Matters as It Is

If some Christians lean toward dualism in their belief about the body (namely, that it is only a temporary shell, or worse, that it is bad or evil), others seem to be overly obsessed with it. Nose jobs, breast implants, adult braces, liposuction, and Botox are commonplace. Our pastor jokes that there's nothing to do in Dallas except work out and get plastic surgery, which is why everyone is so beautiful.

When I first moved to the Dallas area in my late twenties, I came with dreadlocks in my hair and patchouli in my wake. I stuck out like a sore thumb in the land of teased blond hair, perfect noses and teeth, and sculpted bodies. I could not understand the obsession with a seemingly perfect physique—a uniform look almost immediately identifying someone as "from Dallas." I recently saw a photo of a dozen women on social media; they all wore the same outfit (skinny jeans, leather booties, oversized sweaters, and beanies), had the same smiles, displayed the same soft curls in their long balayaged hair, and cocked their knees at just the right angle for prime photo taking. This drive to have a uniform appearance has created an infuriating flatness to the complexity of creation as God designed it. None of us is immune from it

---

[12] C. S. Lewis, *Mere Christianity* (New York: Harper Collins, 2001), 65, emphasis mine.

though. We think that by finding sameness, or friendship, with others, we'll find it within ourselves. The poet Jane Kenyon calls this struggle to find peace with the body a difficult friendship: "This long struggle to be at home / In the body, this difficult friendship."[13] We cannot seem to find peace with the bodies we've been given by God.

This obsession, though, is not actually with the body, as it might seem. The obsession is not care for the body as an embodied self, or an image bearing being. The obsession is being *beyond* the body, beating the body we've been given, adding or subtracting to our substance, pressing back aging and sagging and the effects of bearing babies and hard work. The obsession is not the right care for the body as an image bearing being, but a pursuit of the body of our dreams. What we ultimately want, if we can admit it, is immortality. We desire eternal youth, vitality, beauty, and rigor. The problem is, while those things are coming for us after the resurrection, they aren't going to happen for us on this side of it. Our bodies as they are today—the ones riddled with decay and brokenness and discomfort and frustration—will not live on into eternity. They will get out of the grave and they will change. Living as if we can somehow achieve an immortal, resurrected body now isn't respectful of the person God has made us to be on this side of the earth's story. For the Christian, respecting our body as it is today matters, because it shows we understand we are *not* God, we are *not* infallible or unlimited. We work within the limitations of these bodies for as long as

---

[13] Jane Kenyon, "Cages," *Collected Poems* (St. Paul: Grey Wolf Press, 2005), 36.

we live in them this side of heaven. "Respect for the person is inseparable from respect from the body. . . . A biblical ethic is incarnational. We are made in God's image to reflect God's character, both in our minds and in our bodily actions. There is no division, no alienation. We are embodied beings."[14]

Again, Scripture says those who are in Christ *will* have a new, perfect, and immortal body, but not until we are face-to-face with our God. It's a promise set for the future.

Our world wants to think of our bodies as gods, using tropes like "you're worth it," or "it's our right." But as Christians, we should know it's far more mysterious, glorious, and *ordered* than that. Caring for our bodies to the point of worshipping them is no longer "care" at all. It's idolatry. It's putting our body in the place God should be. There's an order to the way we love things, and God should be our first love. Love and care of our bodies should always go underneath that. God's design for our bodily care is right and good, and the only way we will follow that design is if we love God most. "If affection" of our bodies, as C. S. Lewis wrote, "is made the absolute sovereign of a human life, the seeds will germinate. Love, having become a god, becomes a demon."[15] Saint Augustine's *City of God* was based on the idea that all sin is a result of a disordered love,[16] and this is what self-care—specifically the touching of our bodies as we care for them—has become for many: a disordered love. In this

---

[14] Nancy Pearcey, *Love Thy Body* (Grand Rapids: Baker Publishing, 2018), 34.

[15] C. S. Lewis, *The Four Loves* (New York: Harper One, 2017), 56.

[16] Saint Augustine, *City of God* (New York: Random House, 1993).

way, I can understand why people scoff at the wrong forms of self-care, because the wrong forms of self-care are actually self-worship.

Each of us needs to hear the same message about our bodies, but for different reasons. On one hand, the Christian who thinks their body is bad needs to hear that *their body matters*—it houses the living God! It certainly can't be bad if God dwells in it. On the other hand, the person who treats their body as a god needs to hear the very same message: their body houses the living God, so it cannot be god itself. They need to move their muscles and lift things that feel too heavy at first in order to strengthen their arms for God's good use, not to make them sculpted and toned. They need to eat as though their body was a temple, not to be worshipped, but to house the One they do worship. They need to care for their body not as a god but as a worshipper of the God who made it.

The Necessity of the Everyday Touch

Seeing our bodies as good gifts from God means providing the care they need on a daily basis. This requires touching the body as it is—broken, sagging, wrinkled, freckled, imperfect, love-handled, low-libidoed, or stretch-marked. The touching of *my* body by *me* reminds me of myself and reminds me of God. This personal touch proves my well-being is far more complex and holistic than simply physical health. I need to "feel my substance," as Bessel Van der Kolk says.[17] I need to remember I am a real body created by a real God and my body has real problems that won't be really solved until I'm face-to-face with Him. Touch of self communicates that to us. It reminds us of our own humanity, limitation, and dependence on God. And it points us to the glory of the resurrection awaiting us.

When I stand in front of a mirror massaging moisturizer around the dark circles under my eyes, I am reminded I need to sleep more, or at least get better sleep, because God gives His beloved rest. If I were to stand in front of the mirror in the morning berating myself for the dark circles and avoid touching the cream to my face, not thanking God for sleep or asking Him for better sleep, but instead looking to makeup and Botox and tanning beds to *mask* my need for rest, I would not be caring for the body I have, but some future version of it I want or think is possible. Something as simple as touching my own face with moisturizer can lead me toward God or away from Him.

When I rub the tension from my forearms midday, I remember God is the giver of the gift of writing and I am only a steward who must use it faithfully, which usually means I must take breaks from my work. If I were to refuse to take a moment to massage my overtired forearms, ignoring my body and continuing in the thought that the completion of my work depends on me and not God, I would be caring

---

[17] Krista Tippett, "Bessel van der Kolk, How Trauma Lodges in the Body," *On Being with Krista Tippett*, March 9, 2017, https://onbeing .org/programs/bessel-van-der-kolk-how-trauma-lodges-in-the-body -mar2017/.

for the body I think God wants from me and not the body He's given me.

When I clean my face at the end of the day, rubbing off the dirt it has gathered as I went about my Father's business, I remember the world we live in is grimy and temporal; and then I remember it won't always be. When I brush my teeth, I think of the things that last for ages to come. When I scratch an itch, I remember and give thanks for hands that work and arms that reach and a body that can *feel*. If I were to never wash my face at night or scratch an itch when it comes, I would not be caring for my body at all. I'd be eschewing it, like the dualists, and thinking it unimportant or even sinful.

These little moments of self-touch aren't—or shouldn't be—mindless things. This is the rudimentary work of the body at work in the world. God didn't create humans to be bodiless spirits hovering over the earth. He took dirt and formed man. He took bone and formed woman. He knit us together with material complexity.

As we touch our bodies, we recognize our unique experience and God's unique ability to meet our needs in public and in private. When we touch our bodies with the kind of holistic care God has toward them, we remember our frailty and God's unchangeableness. We remember our weakness and God's strength. We remember we are mere temples, not the God who inhabits them.

The Question of Sexual Self-Touch

A few months ago, I was on a drive with my husband. The topic of our conversation that day was self-touch, masturbation specifically, but mostly it was about paying attention to the natural impulses of our bodies. Our drive took about forty-five minutes and near the beginning of it, I challenged him with something: every time you feel an urge to scratch an itch, push your hair back from your forehead, or readjust how you're sitting, ignore it. For these forty-five minutes, do not obey your body's inclination, desire, or felt need for comfort.

He didn't last five minutes.

Our bodies constantly send us signals about our desires for comfort, help, pleasure, or even medical attention. We are wired by God to pay attention to and care for our bodies. We are knit from conception to move ourselves into comfortable positions, to flinch from pain, and to seek comfort. As we grow, we learn to run from bees and instinctively touch the place where they sting us. We hide from adults who scare us. We learn not to touch the red eye on the stove, and if we happen to do this accidentally, we feel pain and seek to relieve it with ice or ointment. We feel discomfort from old injuries and seek healing or at least respite from them. When we are hungry, we find food. We buy pillows designed for back, side, or belly sleeping—whichever our preference is. We live in a sin-wrecked world with sin-wrecked problems, and comfort is not just a preference, it's a biological instinct—one we're not guaranteed to get while on earth, but one which we'll keep seeking whether we live in a prison cell or a palace. Yes, our ultimate comfort should be found in God alone, but God also built us with physical desires—and solutions—for comfort that aren't always wrong.

God does not have a gift of marriage for everyone, but He does have a gift of singleness for everyone at some point, or at multiple points, in our lives. Most of us will experience a season where we lack a spouse to give relief or release for the biological itch for sexual comfort. Many of us will be in a marriage where mutual relief or release is unavailable for long seasons. How do we operate in that space regarding self-touch without the sin of lust, without the sin of worshipping our felt-desire, or the sin of neglecting the common grace of touch? How does God's design and attentiveness to the body, the necessity of our care for our bodies, submitting ourselves to the biological inclination for comfort and pleasure, and the proclamation against sexual sin inform something like masturbation?

Dear reader, here's the hard news: I do not know.

I think there's something in all of us that wishes there were a rulebook for all the gray areas of Scripture. Maybe it's because we want to control outcomes, or because we're terrified of messing up and going outside the bounds of God's best. In part, I think, it's because we do not trust God to provide our needs or our desires. We believe if we follow a rubric of right and wrong, we can get Him to hear and respond and relent.

In ancient times, when the Bible was written, teens were considered full adults by their culture, and contributed to society as such. There was usually no extended season of waiting for sexual union for a husband or wife in Bible times—by the time hormones and sexual desires peaked, a marriage was already in place. The Bible writers speak to the issues of their day, and while we deal with things like decades of singleness after puberty and cohabitation and masturbation, they were facing sexual contexts like temple prostitution, incest, barrenness, pagan orgies, tribal betrothals, and so on. Their issues of the day were simply different than ours, and we can't expect Bible writers to speak directly to twenty-first century questions, which is one reason the Bible is so silent on masturbation.[18]

Because the Bible is so silent on this issue, it has always been helpful for me to think about prolonged singleness, or times of celibacy, as seasons of fasting—which the Bible *does* speak much about. Paul even talks about married couples fasting from sex for a time.[19] In a long season of celibacy, when the desire for sexual pleasure feels at its peak, it may be helpful to remember that God designed our bodies to be nurtured and cared for—but He also calls Christians to at times fast from what they *feel* they need while still attending to their actual bodily needs. I love the way Eugene Peterson paraphrases Matthew 6:16–18, when Jesus is speaking to His followers about fasting and prayer,

---

[18] There is only one Scripture dealing precisely with what one might call masturbation: Genesis 38:9 (although it was done alongside another person, not in isolation, which is one of the main issues we see playing out today—sexual pleasure divorced from intimacy with a spouse). God disciplines Onan in this passage, not for spilling his semen on the ground, but for not honoring his duty to family and God and giving his dead brother's wife a child.

[19] 1 Corinthians 7:5.

When you practice some appetite-denying discipline to better concentrate on God, don't make a production out of it. It might turn you into a small-time celebrity but it won't make you a saint. If you "go into training" inwardly, act normal outwardly. Shampoo and comb your hair, brush your teeth, wash your face. God doesn't require attention-getting devices. He won't overlook what you are doing; he'll reward you well.[20]

The topic of masturbation—or self-pleasure—is so polarized in our world today, if discussed at all. Depending on whom you talk to (Christian or otherwise), masturbation is either a sin in every case, or some sort of individual sexual right, and therefore completely innocent or even praiseworthy. In the world we often hear, "It's your individual right to take care of yourself however you want, it's your body after all." In the church, we often hear, "Deny, deny, deny!" But what Jesus says in regards to care of bodies and denial of bodily urges is remarkable: He says care and denial are a both/and instead of an either/or—deny *and* care. He says a practice of denying our appetite is good, enabling us to redirect our gaze, heart, desire, body, and mind to the Lord. But at the same time, He says, take care of your body. Your embodied self. He is saying your face matters, your hair matters, your teeth matter, your whole body matters. God hasn't forgotten these felt needs of

---

[20] Eugene Peterson, *The Message: New Testament with Psalms and Proverbs* (Colorado Springs: NavPress, 1995), 19.

your body: in fact, Jesus says, God will not overlook you and will reward you.

Will the reward be marriage? Great sex? Even mediocre sex? At the very least an orgasm experienced in the intimacy of marriage with another? I don't know and you don't know. We don't need to know. God knows and God sees, and not in an evil, conniving, harsh disciplinarian way. In the Christian Standard Bible (csb) translation of this passage, Jesus doesn't say "God." He says, "Your Father." I love that. Your Father, the one who provides all you need and who helps you order your desires rightly and who holds you when you fall and helps you get back up and carries you when the way seems too hard. In a time when you fast from sexual intimacy with another, the Father is still near.

We know this because God came in flesh, dwelt among us, and no temptation known to man was uncommon to Him. *Jesus was in every way tempted as we are yet without sin.*[21] Jesus Christ doesn't just know your desire for comfort or relief; He knows His own. He wept in the garden begging His father to take the cup of suffering from Him. We always follow it quickly to His next words, "Nevertheless, not my will but yours, be done."[22] But we miss something magnificent if we move too quickly. God in flesh, Jesus, the man, wept over His desire for comfort over calling. He bent, prostrate, begging His Father to relent, solve, save, remove, or intervene. We know the end of the story and He did too, and yet He still begged. He knew the temple of His body would

---

[21] Hebrews 4:15.
[22] Luke 22:42.

be raised again in three days, and we know our bodies will be raised with Him in glory. But right now, in many ways, we are living in those three days still. "Birthing is hard / and dying is mean / And living's a trial in between,"[23] the poet Maya Angelou wrote. This living we do sometimes does feel like more suffering than resolving. We are in the "already but not yet"[24] where we are free from sin but not all its effects in this world—we have the ability not to sin, but we still want it sometimes. Knowing that our full freedom is coming, we are still waiting. Groaning. Anticipating. Aching. And sometimes failing and repenting too.

And your Father sees.

Remember Your God in Flesh

"May you keep faith with your body / Learning to see it as a holy sanctuary."[25] As long as we live in the bodies we have (and not the bodies we want to have or someday will have), we will sometimes drink the cup of suffering or decay. We will have circles under our eyes and crooked teeth and love handles and aching muscles and unmet desires. We will have literal itches that need to be scratched and hands that need moisturizer and faces that need to be washed—all by our own hands. Many of us will have strength in our muscles, light

---

[23] Maya Angelou, "Is Love," *The Poetry of Maya Angelou* (New York: Random House, 1993), 234.
[24] Ibid.
[25] John O'Donohue, *To Bless the Space Between Us* (New York: Doubleday, 1998), 61.

in our eyes, mobility to work and explore, and bodies that keep on working for our good—all things we recognize as we touch them with our own hands. We are temples, but not the perfect ornate ones we imagine them to be or want them to be. Our temples are earthly tents, and we get wet when it rains or hot when the temperatures are high or cold when it snows. We are subject to the elements of living on earth. But these tents aren't our home. These biological itches are not the end of us, or the beginning. We're on the way to glory, and our bodies are coming with us, but better, more perfect than we can imagine.

The reminder to the Christian regarding self-touch and the body: Behold, your God in flesh. Behold, your Creator becoming like His creation. Behold, your Savior wrestling with temptation and fear. Behold, your Lord rising again. Behold, your crumbling, cracking, quaking, trembling, itching, comfort-seeking body, one day made new.

CHAPTER FIVE

The Loving Life of Singleness

Have a heart that never hardens,
and a temper that never tires,
and a touch that never hurts.[1]
—Charles Dickens

F or about half the population, marriage will someday be a reality, but for all the world's population, single-ness is a reality at some point—or a few points in life. We will all have a season of singleness, even those who married young. Their season was short and the lessons others learn in extended singleness will have to come to them in different

---

[1] Charles Dickens, *Our Mutual Friend* (New York: Penguin Group, 1997), 434.

ways, but all of us have to learn to navigate the murky waters of aloneness that often accompany being single.

This chapter is not only for those who are single. Feel free to read on if you are single, of course, but this chapter is for all those who have been loved much by God—which is all of us—and all those who want to love God much and others much in return.

The Lonely Edges of Singleness

Nate and I married when I was thirty-four. I'd been schooled in a conservative Christian culture that placed a high value on women becoming wives and mothers as soon as possible—many of my friends were married barely into their twenties or at the end of their teens. When I was twenty-two, thirty-four felt ancient.

As the years passed I felt my singleness more potently. "Maybe this will be the year?" I would journal every January or every birthday. I wanted to be married, I wanted a partner, and I wrongly assumed the desire for a thing meant the certainty of having it eventually. For a time, I believed the well-meaning friends who assured me God had someone for me because He only gives the "gift of singleness to those who feel called to it." As my singleness continued on, I struggled sometimes with the belief that God was good if He didn't give me the gift of marriage.

In the lack of a warm body at my back every night and the fact that I moved nineteen times over a decade and a half, it seemed there was nowhere to lay my head in comfort.

Marriage, for me, felt like the elusive "home" I would never have. I felt a bit like Jesus in Matthew 8:20, "Foxes have holes and birds of the sky have nests, but the Son of Man has no place to lay his head." I was longing for a home for my head, my bed, and my love.

I come from a broken home and know marriage is not a place where opportunity for hurt is rare. And I still wanted the full gamut of marriage. I wanted the good and hard parts of love, the fights and the making up, the baby-making and child-rearing, the growing old together.

What I wanted most of all, though, was to be touched.

I don't mean I just wanted sex—although I wanted that too. What I really longed for was the comfort of a body at my back when I slept and the companionship of my hand in someone else's for the rest of my life. On a hard day I wanted to be like the couple in front of me at church, my shoulder caved into the curve of his arm around my shoulders. I wanted to lean against him in the spaces where I was used to standing alone—at concerts, at a friend's house, in the park, at weddings, and during holidays. I wanted the warmth of a body beside me when I was sick or sad.

Singleness can be a lonely place. And its lonely edges, for many, show up most often around touch and the lack of it. This is where many people *feel* their singleness most potently. It's where I did. Individuals experience singleness in a myriad of ways, but it's around touch that an unmarried person can feel the most forgotten. I polled some singles recently and found agreement—touch was where the lack was felt the most. A few weeks ago a single friend of mine sent me a photo of her and her dog snuggling on the couch: "The saddest and most frequent touch I experience is from Maggie [the dog]. It both makes me supremely happy and terribly sad at the same time."[2]

I shared a story in the introduction from John Piper[3] who spoke of a woman who intentionally cut her body badly enough to need hospitalization on a regular basis. When asked why, she responded, "I like it when they touch me." To many of us that might seem ridiculous, but for one who isn't experiencing healthy touch on a regular basis, the hospital may seem like the most likely place to get it.

Many singles, though in a less extreme manner, feel this same famine of touch. No one touches them in a healthy way. This is rooted in a different problem: singles may feel forgotten in their community. One of the unique aches of singleness is it can feel like, a home aside, there is no place for them anywhere else either. They may feel out of place in churches made up of families, as if there will always be a "plus one" beside their names on wedding invitations or maybe as though no one invites them to their homes for dinner until they're coupled. It feels awkward for a single to press into those places, as though they're an afterthought. It's easier to run to the empty wells of lustful touch or unhealthy touch to try and find sustaining water for the journey of singleness.

---

[2] Text exchange with a friend, used with permission.

[3] John Piper, "How Would You Offer Hope to Someone Who Is Addicted to Cutting Himself?" *Desiring God*, February 9, 2010, https://www.desiringgod.org/interviews/how-would-you-offer-hope-to-someone-who-is-addicted-to-cutting-himself.

You might think I'm going to say singles should press into the difficult spaces where marriages and families find natural fits and give touch to get touch, but I'm not. That would be a manipulation: giving only so one can get. The onus is always on the family of God to touch the marginalized—in this case, the unmarried—not the other way around. The example Jesus sets for us is there were times He put Himself in the way of the marginalized and then *allowed Himself* to be touched by them.

Singles are consistently overlooked in church life, church planning, church leadership, family hospitality, church picnics, and more. We gear ministries toward marriages and families, allocate funds toward marriages and families, hold conferences for marriages and families, and expect singles to babysit, work in the nursery, or just fit themselves in there somewhere. As we leave them out of our plans, we leave them out of our arms. We wave at them from a distance instead of offering a confident and loving embrace, we nod a thank you for watching our children instead of shaking their hand when we pick up our kids from the nursery, we listen to their concerns about life and say "I'll pray for you" instead of placing an affirming hand on their shoulder, or drawing their body to ours for a good, tight, ministering hug, and praying for them in the moment.

When our unmarried brothers and sisters show up to participate in the life of the church, it is an expression of the gospel to recognize their involvement, desire their perspective, and to love them with our touch. To remind them: I see you and know you are a body, a complex person who is not simply a pair of serving hands or missional feet, but an embodied soul who *needs* other embodied souls with whom to mingle. Wendell Berry says it beautifully: "Like divine love, earthly love seeks plenitude; it longs for full membership to be present and to be joined."[4] Unmarried brothers and sisters rightfully long for that plentitude and we, the church family, can give it to them.

Loved Much to Love Much

A few years ago I visited Israel. One of my favorite moments was going into Capernum, going to the synagogue where Jesus once stood and proclaimed: "Today as you listen, this Scripture has been fulfilled."[5] Just a few steps away, though, was a place I loved more: Peter's home.

It is encased now by a modern-looking octagonal building with a glass floor so viewers can look down and see the place where it is believed Jesus slept often, and at the very least taught often. In Mark 1:29–35, it's the place where Jesus healed Peter's mother-in-law, and it's at the door of Peter's house where the whole city gathered to hear Jesus teach, see Him heal the sick, and cast out demons. The man who had no place to lay His head had a place in Peter's home. A mark of the ministry of Jesus was His transience and flexibility, and a mark of the gospel in Peter's life was his hospitality to the transient minister. My friend Jen Pollock Michel in her book,

---

[4] Wendell Berry, *Art of the Commonplace: The Agrarian Essays of Wendell Berry* (Berkley, CA: Counterpoint, 2002), 153.
[5] Luke 4:21.

Keeping Place, wrote this about the gift of having singles in her home as a writer, wife, and mother of five:

> It is not easy to stretch across the demo-
> graphic differences of our lives and make a go
> at community. But this is part of the church's
> housekeeping. If home is God's welcome,
> then each of us must work to make sure
> everyone belongs. God has a home, and he is
> looking to share it. As the psalmist describes
> him, he is "Father to the fatherless and pro-
> tector of widows . . . God settles the solitary
> in a home" (Ps. 68:5–6).[6]

Hospitality is a starting place for how the church family can love our unmarried brothers and sisters, and that's exactly how we should think about it—as the breeding ground of community, the setting for familial interaction. But simply providing a space for people to come or stay or minister out of can also "foster an illusion of relationship and connection." If we aren't careful, it can "disempower and domesticate guests while it reinforces the hosts' power, control, and sense of generosity. It is profoundly destructive to the people it wel-comes. It is the kind of help which, in Philip Hallie's words, 'fills their hands but breaks their hearts.'"[7] While hospitality is good and necessary, there is an intimacy our unmarried

---

[6] Jen Pollock Michel, *Keeping Place* (Downers Grove, IL: InterVarsity Press, 2017), 139.
[7] Christine Pohl, *Making Room: Recovering Hospitality as a Christian Tradition* (Grand Rapids: Eerdmans Publishing Co., 1999), 120.

brothers and sisters need that cannot be met with mere meals and occasional movie nights. For singles to feel connected to the body of believers, healthy touch must be practiced.

We see Jesus in another home in chapter 7 of the book of Luke. He is visiting the home of a Pharisee, and "a woman in the town who was a sinner"—one whose sexual acts were sold for money, some scholars say—came and spilled an alabaster flask of oil over His feet. Scripture says Jesus was reclining and this woman "stood behind him at his feet, weeping, and began to wash his feet with her tears. She wiped his feet with her hair, kissing them and anointing them with the perfume."[8]

The Son of Man was laying at the table of a Pharisee and was touched by a woman who had, many say, gotten paid to lay herself on the beds of men city-wide. If she was, in fact, a prostitute, she was "paid for that which can only be given away."[9] This would have been shocking for plenty of reasons. First, Jesus was a Rabbi, and to be touched by any woman was forbidden, but particularly unclean and sinful women—as this woman would have been deemed. Second, this all happened in the home of a Pharisee, the most legalistic of Jews, to even have a woman of the city in his home would have been problematic.

Yet in the home of the religious elite, Jesus defends the woman's actions and He does it by telling the parable of the money lender who canceled the debt of two men, one who

---

[8] Luke 7:38.

[9] Madeleine L'Engle, "Magdalen," *A Cry Like a Bell* (Wheaton: Harold Shaw Publishers, 1987), 78.

owed little and one who owed much. He asks the Pharisee which of the two would love the moneylender more. "The second, of course," the Pharisee answered. "You're right," Jesus said, "I entered your house; you gave me no water for my feet, but she, with her tears, has washed my feet and wiped them with her hair. You gave me no kiss, but she hasn't stopped kissing my feet since I came in. You didn't anoint my head with olive oil, but she has anointed my feet with perfume. Therefore I tell you, her many sins have been forgiven; that's why she loved much. But the one who is forgiven little, loves little."[10]

And then He said to the woman: "Your sins are forgiven. . . . Your faith has saved you. Go in peace."[11]

Jesus was telling the Pharisees that the mark of a Christian who knows they are loved much is that they love much. In this parable love flows directly back to Jesus, but we know from the rest of Scripture that that love flows all directions. Not only does the loved show a reciprocal love to the one who has forgiven them much, but they also show an initiating love to those around them as well. And in this passage, the one who is loved much, the woman, washes the dirty, grimy, crusty, cracked feet of the one who loves her—the man whose love has flowed all directions as His feet carried Him from city to city, table to table, person to person.

Most interesting is that the woman did not stop touching men after her history—something we'd expect her to do to balance out her past sins. Instead, where she once experienced

---

[10] Luke 7:44–48.
[11] Luke 7:48–50.

the wrong kind of touch in the dark, she was now offering the right kind of touch in the light. She didn't avoid touch; she simply gave it the right way. And the same goes for Jesus— He allowed the right kind of touch. More than allowed, even, He *praised* it. Ministering touch done in the light is a good and glorious thing.

I said at the beginning of this chapter that it was not one for the singles because I think it's tempting for those of us who are married to ignore content about singleness. Maybe it's because we feel like we know it all; maybe it's because we're innately selfish humans, most concerned about what concerns us, but this picture of Jesus and the woman who was loved much *does* concern us. It concerns all of us.

If we are children of God and we know we are loved, then we ought at first to love God. But part of loving God much means generously loving others—particularly those who are marginalized. Like it or not, singles have been marginalized in the church. They're striving toward Christlikeness in a multitude of ways: serving others faithfully, walking around on cracked and bleeding feet, exposing their hearts with love and in love, and rarely finding a place to lay their heads at night that feels like home. And they get up every morning and spread themselves out again in service for the kingdom. I'm not saying they do this perfectly or without moments of weakness, but most faithful singles I know are passionately serving the kingdom of God—or want to be. Yet instead of being brought near as family, they are forgotten, or worse, disregarded by the coupled members of the church sitting around the table. Though they may not be considered unclean or sinful like the woman, they are certainly treated like they don't belong at the table. They are constantly loving much in their service, and yet feel shunned from the community.

Many unmarried people see the beauty of the gift of singleness, and treat it as Elisabeth Elliot said, as "this gift for this day."[11] They love like Jesus loves—widely, broadly, expansively. They live like Jesus in this narrative and are about their Father's business, letting their feet carry them to many homes and churches and places and families and friends and countries. At times they feel dirty, grimy, crusty, and cracked by all they're doing in order to be "concerned about the things of the Lord."[12] They are flexible people who at times feel like there is no place to lay their heads, feeling as though their "hearts are set on pilgrimage,"[13] when what they really want is a home. They feel unfelt at times when they see the physicality that exists in marriages in the form of touch, yes, but they also just long for the concreteness of a house, children, school schedules, and date nights. But if the church body filled with the love of Christ lets that love flow in all directions, those same singles will find themselves at rest for a moment at our tables as part of our lives. In all the unexpected places the Lord takes them, they should encounter the touch of other humans who have been touched by the love of Christ—because they know they are loved and cannot help but to show love back. They will find themselves

---

[11] Elisabeth Elliot, *Let Me Be a Woman* (Wheaton, IL: Tyndale House Publishers, 1976), 31.
[12] 1 Corinthians 7:32.
[13] Psalm 84:5.

in plentitude of touch and feeling the full membership of the living.

⚜ ⚜ ⚜

Maybe that sounds good in principle to you but in practice you are worried. Many of us choose not to include non-family members in the full membership of the living through our touch in order to "abstain from all appearance of evil."[14] But that's a misunderstanding of what God is asking of us as His people. Think again about the example of Jesus in this Pharisee's house as He welcomed the woman of the city. This wasn't a "safe" space for touch. If anything, this was the least safe space for Jesus to allow Himself to be touched by a woman of the city. What would these people think? If it was the home of one of His friends, it would have been safer from prying eyes. In the home of the Pharisee, though, who knew what stories were spread after this moment? Jesus and the woman didn't act with ultimate allegiance to the version of events that would be spread about them, they acted upon what was right and godly. In other words, they acted just as one who loves much and one who received that love *should* act.

When it comes to our single friends in the church, instead of prioritizing the keeping up of appearances, what might it look like for married people to prioritize giving them the gift of physical touch in appropriate but very intentional

---

[14] 1 Thessalonians 5:22 (KJV). Better translated in CSB as "Stay away from every kind of evil."

ways? The woman heard Jesus was in the home of the Pharisee, gathered her expensive oil, and came in an inglorious way to serve her King. She showed her love by crawling up behind the one who served much, taking His feet in her hands, washing them, anointing them, and kissing them. She was not looking for glory or fame or money or even notice. She brought nothing to Jesus except her touch. This was no quick side hug in the foyer of the local synagogue. It was no quick hand on the shoulder in the coffee shop. It was sacrificial, intentional, exorbitant, and carried the risk of public humiliation. It was dirty work. But she did it anyway. She found Jesus in a moment of seeming rest from His work and touched Him.

Let the Light Reign

In a conversation about this book, William Jensen (my literary agent and friend) said one of the more profound statements I've heard and one which has always been in my mind since: "We want our souls to mingle, but our bodies keep getting in the way." He's profoundly right, but what if we stopped thinking of our bodies as something in the way? What if we stopped thinking of the body God created as our main obstacle to intimacy with others or even the only means to intimacy? If we did, we could begin broadening our concepts of healthy intimacy to the inclusion of our bodies and others' bodies in non-sexual ways.

Whether you are single or married, if you are a child of God, you are loved much. Go and love the singles in your life much. Ask them if they are receiving healthy physical touch from anyone in their lives. Don't ever assume an unmarried person is being touched in appropriate ways somewhere else in their lives. It is more likely that they have been touched or are touching inappropriately in dating relationships or friendships, or they are using self-touch to pacify their deep need for physical touch. It is rare to find an unmarried person who isn't using one or both of these mechanisms to offer themselves solace. When we assume *wrongly* that they're being touched healthily in other places, we press them further back into sinful expressions of touch.

If they're not receiving healthy touch, and your intentions for them are pure, ask them if you can hug them. Sit near them at church and, if it's appropriate, lend your shoulder to be leaned upon. Lay your hands on them in prayer. Hug them well when you see them. Did you know it takes eight seconds of hugging for endorphins to be released in our bodies? For an unmarried person who is rarely being touched, those endorphins might be the only ones released through touch for them that day.

I often ask my close friends who are unmarried, "When was the last time you were hugged?" And then I hug them, male and female, tightly and indiscriminately. Sometimes it's the only touch they get all week. One of the many single guys in our small group from church who meets in our home each week says often, "One of my favorite parts of home-group is knowing I'm going to give and get so many hugs all evening. It's the most touch I get all week." He works in a Christian environment, surrounded by Christians all week, and yet the only physical touch he ever experiences is within two hours, one night a week. This shouldn't be.

When you stand across from an unmarried person, remember: you're called to be faithful to the Lord and to care for the person in front of you, not the outcome or narrative you want told about you. Your aim should be Christlikeness, and Christ gave touch in loving and appropriate ways, and He received it likewise.

The Bible may not tell us exactly how to interact with other bodies, but it does show us one way: by giving a home to the homeless and offering appropriate touch within that space. By following Jesus' example and including the married and the single in our healthy touch, we can break down the barriers in the body of Christ and foster a more life-giving experience for its members. For where touch is done in the light, as it is in this example of Jesus at the house of the Pharisee, the light reigns. When you walk away from caring for a marginalized, unmarried person through faithful, loving, serving touch, you can, like the woman in Luke 7, go in peace. It is not your touch that saves you *or* condemns you, it is your faith in the one who loves you much.

CHAPTER SIX

Opposites Don't Always Attract

*When we honestly ask ourselves which person
in our lives means the most to us, we often
find that it is those who—instead of giving
advice, solutions, or cures—have chosen rather
to share our pain and touch our wounds with
a warm and tender hand.*[1]
—Henri Nouwen

I grew up in mostly non-denominational or Protestant churches in Bucks County, Pennsylvania. My hometown was called Quakertown—an area brimming over with practicing Quakers, as well as newer order Mennonites. The

---

[1] Henri Nouwen, *Out of Solitude: Three Meditations on the Christian Life* (Notre Dame, IN: Ave Marie Press, 2008), 38.

Shaker influence of having nothing superfluous was a bench-
mark of the communities in this area. Churches were sparsely
decorated: white walls, with large, many-paned windows
with the trademark historic deep window-sills of buildings
established in the 1700s and 1800s. When I would attend
Mass with my Catholic grandparents, I was enraptured by
the stained-glass windows adorning their cathedral, standing
in vivid contrast to the surrounding minimalism to which I
was accustomed.

There was one Catholic chapel, though, that set itself
apart, combining the modesty of the historical area with
the beauty of stained glass. It was set on top of a hill near
a U-Pick strawberry patch we frequented in the summers.
From the outside, the chapel was austere and plain, dark
brown clapboard with a weathered steeple. Inside, the walls
were white, the pews brown, blending in with the wood
floor and providing an unobstructed view of the magnificent
stained-glass windows surrounding them. Because the chapel
was high on a hill and there was nothing else about the building vying for one's attention, the light streamed brilliantly in
those windows creating one of the most memorable sights I
have ever seen.

I was only nine years old when one particular window in
that chapel made an impression I have never forgotten. Jesus
was centered in the frame, wearing blue, with the trademark
halo backing Him. Across His chest lay a man in red, his
eyes drooping in sleep, the hand of Jesus cupping his shoulder. Jesus' other hand was raised in blessing, or teaching, or

waving—I never knew. There was no one else portrayed in this particular window, or if there was, I never noticed.

I liked *this* Jesus. The Jesus I knew about had all kinds of rules and demands I could never meet. But *this* Jesus seemed like a friend I would want—comforting, protective, and confident. And this man reclining across his chest seemed like the sort of person I wanted to be—loved, relaxed, and safe.

It would be years before I equated John, the disciple whom Jesus loved, with the man wearing red in the window. But whenever I think of being one who Jesus loves, I think of that stained-glass window in the hilltop chapel. This is what it means to be loved as a friend: brilliant and beautiful and, at the very least, it means to be touched with care.

In our culture, including our church culture, the kind of touch between close friends that's depicted in the stained-glass window would be construed as something more than friendship because we have infused all touch between friends, of the same or opposite sex, with sexual meaning. This is where the common terms like "bromance" come from—we don't know how to interpret true and deep friendships, so we attach some sort of romantic or sexualized love to them. Sam Allberry, a man who has wrestled with his singleness, sexuality, and intimacy in friendship, has written, "Our Western culture has so identified sex and intimacy that in popular thinking the two are virtually identical. We cannot conceive of intimacy occurring without it in some way being sexual. So when we hear how previous generations described friendship in such intimate terms, we roll our eyes and say, 'Well they were obviously gay.' Any intimacy, we imagine, must ultimately be sexual."[2]

These thoughts and questions permeate our friendships, both in opposite gender friendships, and increasingly in same gender friendships among Christians—and if they go unexamined or unquestioned they keep us from healthy and necessary touch with one another.

Opposites Don't Always Attract

This fall I will be twice a bridesmaid. The second is the wedding of our current housemate, who was also my room-mate before I got married. The first is the wedding of one of my oldest and dearest friends. We haven't seen much of one another since their engagement this summer, but our friend-ship is nearly a decade old, and while marriage will change a lot of things, it won't change our deep love and affection for one another. In some of my most difficult moments over the past nearly ten years, this friend has been there, listen-ing, asking questions, saying hard things, and is one of the best huggers I know. When I'm being hugged by him, I know he loves me. His embrace is strong, firm, using two arms, enveloping, and probably five or six seconds longer than hugs with most people I know. And, which is more, I see the same indiscriminate hug being offered to everyone who comes across his path. He'll be the first to say he loves

[2] Sam Allberry, "Why Single Is Not the Same as Lonely," The Gospel Coalition, July 11, 2016, 6, https://www.thegospelcoalition.org /article/why-single-is-not-same-as-lonely/.

to both receive and give physical touch. Watching him navigate this now as an engaged—soon to be married—man, and stepfather to two little ones, is a great joy for me.

My friend was also the one who first introduced my husband, Nate, to me in the foyer of our local church. I found out later Nate made the assumption that because of our closeness and familiarity with one another, the presence of a hand on a shoulder or arm, or a good, tight hug, that my friend was interested in me. When he asked my friend about it, though, there was no disgust in his response or jovial joking as bros, he simply said, "Nope, she's just one of my best friends." Beyond any doubt, our affection for one another is and always has been purely platonic. We've had candid conversations about the lack of physical attraction for one another and yet the presence of deep love and affection, and marveled at God's gift of friendship in it. I imagine Nate isn't the only one to have made this assumption about my friend and me over the years. I know our opposite gender friendship is, perhaps, an exception to the rule within the church, but I wish it wasn't.

Aimee Byrd in her excellent book *Why Can't We Be Friends* (which has the brilliant subtitle *Avoidance Is Not Purity*) says, "Decades before *When Harry Met Sally* came out, [positing that men and women couldn't be friends because "the sex part always gets in the way"], Sigmund Freud reduced all affection to erotic desires—to our genitals— meaning that every look, gesture, touch, and thought holds sexual motives."[3] She has written an entire book refuting this

---

[3] Aimee Byrd, *Why Can't We Be Friends* (Phillipsburg, NJ: P&R Publishing, 2018), 35.

biblically—and I recommend you read it—where she also says, "The church has accepted and semi-sanctified these reductive views: sexuality is good for landing a spouse, but it's a barrier to friendship because men and women can't possibly just enjoy one another's company. We associate all intimacy with the bedroom between a man and woman to be laden with repressed sexual desire. That means that all intellectual, creative, entertaining, or conversational enjoyment with someone of the other sex needs to be fulfilled by our spouses. That's an awfully heavy load for one person to bear."[4]

Too often we support that burden bearing by using tropes, fears, quips, and clichés to dictate what we do with our hands. I saw this happening when I noticed a dear pastor friend of mine refused to hug any woman ever—even from the side. Eventually I asked him why he wasn't hugging the women in his congregation and he said, "Well, my wife was touched sinfully by a pastor when she was in high school and I just never want to give her a reason to suspect me of doing the same to other women."

I thought about his words for a few weeks. I could see his good intentions and posture toward his wife, but I also had a few questions so I followed back up with him: "Have you considered the possibility that you may need to speak and care for your wife by helping her to see that while she was sinned against, not every man has the same intention or heart? And have you asked if you are submitting to your wife's fear above God's intention for caring for His sheep, and in being mastered by your wife's fear, if you alienate the

---

[4] Ibid.

women in your care as a pastor and leave them feeling like a potential threat to your wife's peace? Or, assuming they don't even *know* why you refrain from hugging them, it is possible that they assume *they* are the reason? As though they are a threat to your body or ministry? And lastly, have you weighed the risk that you are doing an opposite but just as harmful action to women in your church by not interacting with them in faithful, humble, godly touch?"

When we set up boundaries like "I'll never hug a person of the opposite sex" as a reaction to present fears or possible outcomes, we are not being faithful to the ways of Jesus, but being driven by weak arguments, unresolved personal histories, or "What ifs?" That's not the way of the Christian. Christians should have their eyes set on the flourishing of all people, to withhold a good thing from an entire gender class as a precautionary measure keeps us from the goal of human flourishing. A Christian obeys Jesus' example as seen in God's Word, trusting God will heal and help us overcome fears, and we will do the right thing regardless of the outcome.

Because we have infused sexual meaning into all levels of intimacy within our relationships between opposite genders, we have made the healthy touch we are created for a burden for spouses who should not bear it alone, and an increasing rarity for singles.

Same-Sex Friendship Is Meant to Be Comforting, Not Confusing

It isn't just male-female relationships that suffer from the infusion of sexual meaning into friendship. Our current culture is all over the spectrum in its views on same-sex relationships—everything from the affirmation and celebration of gay marriage on one side, to a squeamish or even vitriolic distaste for any affection or touch among friends of the same gender on the other.

I moved out of my parents' home in the infancy of their divorce. Their marriage hadn't been good for years, and our family was still in the stupors of grief following the sudden and accidental death of my fourteen-year-old brother. We were the definition of the walking wounded. Most nights I cried myself to sleep. I was desperate for safe and comforting touch.

The home I moved into was with three other girls. We were all affectionate with one another to varying degrees, but I felt a raw hunger at times that seemed to gnaw within me. I was twenty, single, in an environment where affection between opposite-sex friends was awkward or unpracticed, and affection between same-sex friends was always assumed to be good or pure.

One of my roommates was nearly a decade older than me, a sister I'd never had, and was voraciously affectionate with me. She had lost her mother at a young age and knew some of the grief I was walking through. She became, for me, a safe home. She held me when I wept. She taught me to care for my body and soul in a time when no one was caring for it at all—she was the first person who showed me how to tweeze my eyebrows and taught me the wonder of taking a bath by candlelight alone at the end of a long day. She would hug me tight and directly. And, I observed, she did the same with all my brothers. Her love for me matched her love for them and her expressions of her love matched too. She was indiscriminate in her physical touch. It was profoundly healing for me and for my whole family. The question of attraction to her was never one in my mind. She was my sister, my *friend*. That's all.

I wrote in chapter 1 about how I lived with a total of thirty-eight roommates over the years and how I began to see this physical affection and closeness that seemed so safe to me was a place of confusion for some. Girls who grew up dreaming about boyfriends and husbands were thrown into identity crises around their sexuality because comfortable, acceptable touch turned sexually intimate.

Interestingly, on the other side of the spectrum, there are expressions of touch between friends that are expressly dedicated to communicating that there is *zero sexual attraction here*. It's been long noticed in white contexts that this sort of thing particularly shows up in the "bro-hug" (which can sometimes incorporate three pats on the back) that communicates to the huggers and to the world, "I'm. Not. Gay." This has literally been called the "I'm not gay" hug since dating back to 2007.[5] More interesting is that these types of signals aren't necessary in many other cultural contexts where

---

[5] https://www.urbandictionary.com/define.php?term=%22im%20not%20gay%22%20hug.

two people of the same sex interact physically in friendship. In Asian, African, European, and many other cultures, for instance, it's customary for platonic friends to hold hands or kiss each other on the cheek as a form of affection, where the affection is simply that—affection. It's not a *signal* to one another or the world about *not being attracted*. It's merely a display of love and honor and warmth within friendship, much like Peter tells us to do in the New Testament with one another, and many characters in the Old Testament do with one another as well. Within modern American (and usually white) culture, though, the confusion is rampant and most of us are too quick to ask, "Am I attracted to you?" instead of "How do I touch in a way that is intimate, pure, sincere, and godly?"

Regardless of whether we are in a same-sex or opposite-sex friendship, it's obvious that we are all still stuck in the Freudian cycle of belief that all touch is erotic. Even when I mentioned writing this book, the erotic forms of touch were all anyone asked about. We are so sexualized in our culture that we cannot divorce erotic touch from faithful, ministerial touch with those between whom there is no physical attraction.

The church certainly doesn't help, either. Aimee Byrd again says,

> As eager as the conservative church is to speak
> out against the sexual revolution and gender
> identity theories, she often appears just as
> reductive as the culture surrounding her when
> it comes to representing our communion with

God in our communion with one another.
But Scripture tells us over and over again
that Christian men and women are more than
friends—we are brothers and sisters in Christ.
Paul tells Timothy to treat gender distinction
in a familiar way. He petitions him to appeal
to the older men as fathers, "the younger men
as brothers, the older women as mothers, and
the younger women as sisters, in all purity."[6]
This says it all. Paul doesn't give Timothy a
bunch of details on how to treat a father or a
sister; we already know how to do that. It's a
respectful way to relate to one another—and,
when we relate this way, we remove the possibility of sex.[7]

How do we live, then, in a world mashed up against
billions of other human beings who will not be or are not
presently our spouse? We cannot and should not avoid touch
between same genders or opposite genders, so how do we
touch faithfully as friends?

Be Loved

We know the gospel is primarily about being and not
doing, although the result of being—abiding in Christ, obey-
ing the Spirit inside us, accepting the love of our Father—will

---

[6] 1 Timothy 5:1–2.
[7] Aimee Byrd, *Why Can't We Be Friends*, 14.

result in a changed heart and actions. We will never *be* perfect until the resurrection; until then, it is an ongoing work of the Holy Spirit for the rest of our lives. But the assumption of *being* loved by God will change the way we interact with others in every way, including touch.

Think again about the stained-glass window depicting the disciple reclining across Jesus. The beloved disciple knew he was loved by Jesus. I used to think he mentioned twice in his Gospel that he reclined across the chest of Jesus at the last supper because he wanted to prove to his readers that Jesus loved him best. Like the kid who can't stop bragging to anyone who will listen that he's his dad's favorite kid. But as I learn more about abiding in Christ—and how much ink John gave in his narrative to Christ's words about abiding[8]—the more I think John wasn't trying to prove anything to anyone. Telling us of his physical closeness to Jesus at the Last Supper and again before the Transfiguration was assurance and hope to his readers: this intimate friendship is the kind of love Jesus has for those who rest in His love for them, this physical close-ness is what's possible for those who stay connected to the love God gives them. This closeness is the gift of those who abide.

❄ ❄ ❄

We tend to feel better with clear rules and regulations, so much so that we lean on verses out of context to create strict boundaries of right and wrong where they don't exist. First Corinthians 7:1–2 is often translated as, "It's not good for a

---

[8] John 15.

man to touch a woman," but Paul isn't referring to mere touch as brothers and sisters, but the use of a woman for sexual touch outside marriage. The Christian Standard Bible (csb) translates it as, "'It is good for a man not to use a woman for sex.' But because sexual immorality is so common, each man should have sexual relations with his own wife, and each woman should have sexual relations with her own husband." The New Testament sets a wide perimeter around what is acceptable touch between brothers and brothers, sisters and sisters, and brothers and sisters—mostly portrayed through descriptive accounts, but some prescriptive. (Greet everyone with a holy kiss,[9] would be one example.)

Instead of creating deep appreciation for what God has given us as brothers and sisters, much of Christian culture plants its flag in the ground of mere impressions, but that is muddy ground indeed. As I mentioned in the previous chapter, many will express a worry of what others think of them as the reason for much of the confusion around touch between friends—same gender or opposite gender. This confusion grows not from a root of fear of what others will think, though, but from a lack of assurance about what God thinks, namely that we are loved by Him. Living in assurance that God loves us frees us from the fear of other people's assumptions. If we are loved by God, then what does it matter what someone assumes about us? If we are loved by God, doesn't it free us up to walk faithfully, navigate difficult things, and still abide sweetly in Him? Yes, we should obviously live above reproach, but that happens naturally when we are

---

[9] Romans 16:16; 1 Corinthians 16:20.

abiding in God's love for us. And living above reproach is not synonymous with keeping a six-foot distance between yourself and other humans.

A few weeks ago I had a conversation over this chapter with a mother who had a different perspective. She protested that her sons could get the wrong impression if a girl hugged them or touched them even *with* pure intentions and motives. She had instructed her sons to "only give side hugs," a one-armed press and quick pat, and quickly withdraw. She was just as concerned the girls would get the wrong impression. "We just have to make sure people don't assume." I hear her sentiment; she wants what's best for everyone. But Scripture makes it clear again and again that we cannot control the minds, actions, or assumptions of others—that the fear of man is a certain trap.[10]

If my fear about touching a friend begins as a thought in my mind, *What will they think?* then I have already betrayed my lack of belief in God's love for me that drives me to love others. If I truly believe God loves me and I abide in that love, then what people *think* of whether I greet another with a full hug or handshake, will matter less and less to me: I know whose opinion of me matters most. Our call is not to "make sure," our only call is to faithfulness. We are faithful first to what God has asked of us and second, by having care toward the person in front of us. Our question, therefore, should not be, "What will they think?" but "How can I best care for them in this moment?" Perhaps the one standing before us has a history of being abused, or a history of false accusation,

---

[10] Proverbs 29:25.

or a physical disability, or any number of complicating factors. Asking the question, "What would be the most caring way I can engage with them physically right now?" will help us grow in empathy, care, and maturity.

David Linden, in an interview with *The Atlantic*, said, "Anytime you make a rule, you have to think about what's lost, and what's lost when touch is forbidden is important." The article described the school his children attended, "Where touch is not only allowed, it's also an essential part of the school's philosophy. 'One of the things I love about my kids' school is that the kids are all over each other.[11] The school made it clear from the first day that if we don't want our children to be touched, this isn't the school for them. I'm grateful for that, because my children have been raised to understand that touch isn't just for sex, it's an affiliative thing you do to bond with other human beings."[12] When we restrict touch between friends because we only equate it to erotic touch, we do children a disservice for their future. They will wrestle to undo the tight web of belief that all touch is erotic for the rest of their lives. Maybe someone might get the wrong impression sometimes, but that can be good in the

---

[11] It's important to note that sometimes "kids being all over each other" can lead to early experimentation with sexual touch (as in my own case), and so it is deeply necessary that we implement adult supervision wherever we want to cultivate atmospheres of healthy physical touch amongst those too immature to know the nuances between healthy and unhealthy.
[12] Jessica Lahey, "Should Teachers Be Allowed to Touch Students?" *The Atlantic*, January 23, 2015, https://www.theatlantic.com/education /archive/2015/01/the-benefits-of-touch/384706/?fbclid=IwAR1W_dRJ YVKN1wBeX7DGkbHh1FLrwQvyRh15jV20p34gThS9O0y0eMMT 8_Y.

end—it shows that not all touch is sexual, and corrects the person who interprets every instance of touch that way.

No one can navigate the bog of how long a hug should last. How tight? Should it be front or side? It's far too subjective to create laws where God doesn't set them. For some people in certain situations, it may be loving, appropriate, and godly to let a hug linger. For others in different situations, it may not be. As we raise children and as we practice Christian friendship as brothers and sisters, we want to be faithful to and encourage faithfulness to Scripture and not faithfulness to the mere possibility or even probability of wrong impressions.

※ ※ ※

Knowing we are loved by Christ also frees us from finding our identity in what we get from others in their touch. If I have a friend who isn't comfortable hugging, that says nothing about me, but them. Maybe they're someone who hasn't healed from a false accusation from someone else, or who sinfully fears a false accusation to come. Maybe they're someone who experienced trauma and being hugged tightly makes them feel unsafe. Maybe they're a child with disabilities and touch is difficult for them. Maybe they have a debilitating illness that causes pain when they're touched. Maybe they struggle with their body image and being hugged feels embarrassing. All of those stories matter infinitely to our infinite God, but they're not about me at all. Abiding in the knowledge of God's love for me, being beloved, frees me to care about them and their story, and not what their fear of touching me says about me. As C. S. Lewis says, "Friendship is utterly free from Affection's need to be needed."[13]

When we know we are loved, it frees us to love indiscriminately, getting nothing in return, only giving freely—and even being free to have our touch or love rejected. Our worth is not in how someone receives or rejects our love. "If you are hidden with Christ in God, then you have nothing more to hide. You are free to be you. The real you."[14]

Freed to Touch and Be Touched

In areas where Scripture isn't clear, we have to discern the Spirit's prompting, and then walk in faithfulness therein. Whether people get the wrong impression or not is not within our control. My husband and I say often to one another: "We cannot play chess with people or relationships; our only call is to be faithful to the Word of God." So how do we wisely navigate the bog of touch within friendship between the same gender or between different genders in a world that assumes eroticism in most touch?

We abide in the truth that we are infinitely loved by God and the loving way to interact physically with any human, male or female, young or old, is to care more about the other than we do ourselves. Don't set rules or measures about hugging the opposite gender or the same gender—view all people

[13] C. S. Lewis, *The Four Loves* (New York: Harper One, 2017), 69.
[14] Jared Wilson, *The Imperfect Disciple* (Grand Rapids: Baker Books, 2017), 190.

as image bearers of the Most High, with complicated and beautiful stories all intended by our Creator to show us His infinite love.

For men and women who slink back into themselves or their marriage alone for touch, see your brothers and sisters as disciples whom Jesus loves and enact that love toward them in appropriate life-giving touch. A side hug between friends says there's fear of being more than just friends instead of trust and appreciation.

Rest assured that the one loved by God is free to hug however the person coming toward them hugs—his worth isn't in whether she goes in for a side hug or he holds out his hand or does nothing at all. Her worth isn't in whether he's afraid of front-hugging or hugs a bit tighter than expected. His fear of her or his lingering hug is about him, not her. She can still sleep at night knowing she is loved by God.

For unmarried singles who are seeking to honor God with their bodies and yet long for healthy, human touch, find that touch within your friendships with men *and* women. You may feel the ache of desire for sex potent within you often, but more times than not, the ache shows up earlier in the simple need for loving human touch. Ask for it and give it freely. You are loved by the Christ, Son of the living God.

I am a disciple whom Jesus loves. And if you're a follower of Christ, you're a disciple whom Jesus loves, and this frees you to touch the one who loves you and whom you love in return freely, purely, and intentionally—as the brother or sister in Christ they are.

CHAPTER SEVEN

True Love Doesn't Wait to Touch

Touch me,
remind me who I am.[1]
—Stanley Kunitz

Human love is directed to the other
person for his own sake, spiritual love
loves him for Christ's sake.[2]
—Dietrich Bonhoeffer

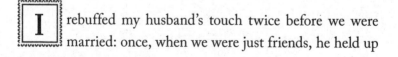 rebuffed my husband's touch twice before we were married: once, when we were just friends, he held up

---

[1] Stanley Kunitz, "Touch Me" in *Passing Through: The Later Poems* (New York: W. W. Norton & Company, 1995), 158–59.
[2] Dietrich Bonhoeffer, *Life Together* (New York: Harper & Row Publishers, Inc., Harper Collins, 1954), 34.

his fist for a "fist bump" because we agreed about something. I looked at it and said, "I'm not one of your *bros*, I'm not going to 'fist bump' you." He might have fallen in like with me a little right then. The second was our first kiss. He went in for it; it was the last thing I expected in that moment, and I turned my head to the side.

We laugh about both memories now. It might sound like I was a prude, but I wasn't. It was that I didn't want to be in the same category as his guy friends; I wanted to be his *girlfriend*. The first kiss is a longer story (maybe I'll tell you someday, but suffice it to say we kiss just fine now).

The Promises of the Purity Culture

I grew up a product of the Purity Movement of the '90s and early 2000s, the popular era of courtship, True Love Waits rallies, and promise rings. But no promise to make True Love Wait kept me from sampling the appetizers for the feast I envisioned sex to be. My first kiss happened when I was thirteen. I recorded its momentous occasion in a small diary and taped in a heart-shaped leaf I'd found on the same road where the kiss happened. It didn't take long for that kiss to lead to fumbling hands under our clothing, taking what we could of one another's bodies. We were still kids on the outside, playing hide-and-seek with our siblings, but we'd hide together in the darkest corners we could find and make out until we were found out. This began a decades-long wrestle inside me in regard to touch within dating relationships. I did not date often, but when I did, I could not find a middle ground: my relationships were built almost entirely on touch or completely void of physical touch. I wasn't committed to True Love Waiting as much as I was the *appearance of purity* or, when that failed, to the selfish seeking of my own pleasure. I don't think I'm alone here.

Sin is bound up in the heart of every child and while I make no excuse for my behavior, I know part of my actions were due to an under-developed (or even wrongly developed) understanding of purity, sex, and touch in general. I'd been given a book by my parents when I expressed curiosity about a particularly coarse word I'd heard at school in first or second grade, and that was all the information I had. And it was simply that—information. It was phrased as though sex was something only mommies and daddies did, and its sole purpose was to make babies.

What, then, was a thirteen-year-old to do with these newfound feelings, fears, desires, and fumbling hands? The only thing I knew about sex apart from the biological act, was people said it was guaranteed to be better if you waited until marriage to have it. But "better" is a difficult thing to understand whether you're talking about ice cream flavors, summer vacation, or sex. "Better" is a concrete thing; it's not abstract. It *means* something; it's something *above* something else. And it presupposes familiarity with the *lesser* thing in order to compare. I assumed people were right about sex being better someday, but also saw no problem sampling the less good until the better was possible.

When I reached my late teens and into my twenties, I was immersed in the culture that "kissed dating goodbye."[3] My peers and leaders at that time were enthralled with *courtship* and its practices, waiting to kiss until the altar, priding ourselves with purity. Some of my friends didn't even hold hands until their wedding day. The assumption was we weren't having sex and we weren't even thinking about having it. It was commonplace to hear talk about giving away "pieces of our hearts" or stealing touch from someone else's future spouse. We collectively believed marriage was equal parts a reward for good behavior and would only come for us when we were "ready." Though what "ready" was, nobody could say. The assumption was that God would give you the right person when you had proven you were prepared for the responsibility of commitment.[4] The problem with this wasn't the desire to show that marriage requires responsibility and commitment; after all, that's very true. The problem was that the movement was driven by pride and fear: fear of overstepping the "line" and pride when a couple "saved themselves for marriage." When courtships ended without the intended goal of marriage, instead of resulting in healthy introspection and greater self-awareness, they usually resulted in copious amounts of shame, mistrust of and in future relationships, and more. If your first courtship experience didn't pan out

---

[3] *I Kissed Dating Goodbye* was a bestseller written by twenty-one-year-old (at the time) Joshua Harris. Now in his forties, he's since stopped its publication, and repented to a generation of conservative Christian kids (and their well-meaning parents) who swallowed its message without question.
[4] Joshua Harris, *I Kissed Dating Goodbye* (Colorado Springs: Multnomah Press, 1997, 2003) 86.

well, your entire community would consider you damaged goods, saying, "'Oh, that person gave their heart away.'"[5]

The lofty goal of "not giving your heart away" straitjacketed the dating culture within the church, not just around dating but around touch within dating as well. The aim was marriage, and if not marriage, then at least not getting your heart broken, and certainly not doing anything you wouldn't tell your youth pastor about. Premarital sex, kissing, touching, holding hands, all of it equaled a broken heart that equaled regrets. "Regret" was the scariest word, though, like "better," nobody knew what it was until they had it. All I can remember is that the regret had to do with how damaged you'd be, and that if you failed at any point, you'd forfeit your chance at a spouse or a good marriage. While the desire to enter in a healthy marriage is not a bad desire, again, the problem with the whole purity movement was that *getting the relationship* was idolized instead of God.

Telling the Truth with Our Bodies

What would have been more helpful for me at twelve years old, as well as at fifteen, twenty, twenty-five, or thirty, was to understand my fidelity was not primarily to a future spouse or to a purity movement. My fidelity was to the God who made my body for my good and His glory.

---

[5] Jessica Van Der Wyngaard and Joshua Harris, *I Survived I Kissed Dating Goodbye*, documentary, 2018.

Contrary to phrases like "The joy of intimacy is the reward of commitment,"[6] sex is not *necessarily* better because we wait for it or because we only do it within marriage. And even if we do wait for it or constrain it to marriage, it still has plenty of opportunity for confusion, fear, sin, and more. The *better*ness of sex within marriage is an ancillary point. Purity is not the prize we come to marriage bearing. Virginity or white-knuckling our desires throughout singleness is not the aim. Marriage itself is not even the aim. We're not promised marriage, nor are we promised sex within marriage, nor are we promised great sex within marriage. Our desire should be to walk in purity, faithfulness, and submission to God's best for us in both singleness and marriage, if God gives it to us. Rachel Joy Welcher says it well: "God never treats sex as a reward. If it were, all the godly, chaste men and women we know would be married right now, having mind-blowing sex and making lots of beautiful babies without any struggles with illness or infertility. If sex were a reward, then our friends who live with their boyfriends and girlfriends would all be impotent or having terrible sex." She's right, and goes on: "The biblical truth is that practicing sexual abstinence doesn't guarantee marriage or crazy-awesome sex any more than taking up our cross and following Christ guarantees us health, wealth, or happiness."[7]

---

[6] Joshua Harris, *I Kissed Dating Goodbye* (Colorado Springs: Multnomah Press, 1997, 2003), 25.

[7] Rachel Joy Welcher, *Talking Back to Purity Culture* (unpublished as of yet).

※ ※ ※

Like the 1 Corinthians 7:1–2 verses we looked at in the last chapter, Christians lean on poorly translated verses taken out of context to create laws and boundaries around touch before marriage. Verses like, "It's good for a man to not touch a woman," are firmly inserted into friendships and dating relationships to draw hard lines. We saw that the CSB translates that verse as, "It is good for a man not to use a woman for sex," which, in context of the chapter about proper relationships, makes far more sense. It wouldn't have made sense for Paul to refuse what Christ had encouraged (closing the gaps previously made by Levitical law) or what he *himself* instructed in other letters (to love one another with brotherly affection and holy touch in Rom. 12:10; 16:16).

But how close is too close? Certainly the world's rubric for casual sex—and touch intended to incite sexual responses—isn't honoring to God *or* to our bodies. Nancy Pearcey, in her book *Love Thy Body* quotes Tim Keller, "'Sex is God's appointed way for two people to say reciprocally to one another, 'I belong completely, permanently, and exclusively to you.'"[8] She then goes on to say, "when we have sex outside of marriage, we are essentially lying with our bodies. Our actions are 'saying' that we are united on all levels when in

---

[8] Tim and Kathy Keller, *The Meaning of Marriage* (New York: Dutton, a Penguin Group, 2011), 257.

reality, we are not. We are contradicting ourselves. We are putting on an act. We are being dishonest."[9]

The question then, for the Christian, is how *does* one engage touch in a faithful, God-honoring, Spirit-fueled way in romantic relationships before marriage? How do we touch in a way that honors God and the other, that isn't taking a thing before it's time, and that isn't a list of rules adhered to in hopes that if we follow them, we'll have exactly what we want later and it will be "better"? How do we bear the fruit of the Spirit toward one another while still expressing the good, God-honoring gift of touch? In short, how do we tell the truth with our touch?

Work Toward the Future We Know, Not Just the Future We Want

Much of the confusion about touch in dating or engagement stems not only from our innate desire for instant gratification, but the confusing narrative we're given within the church and the world. Western hookup culture makes nothing of one-night stands, late-night calls for "Netflix and chill," and other kinds of damaging touch for sexual gratification. There is little talk about limitations or boundaries; the assumption is if one wants it, they can take it or give it. There is little talk, all action.

The pendulum swing within the church mostly congregates around how much is too much, too long, or too

---

[9] Nancy Pearcey, *Love Thy Body* (Grand Rapids: Baker Publishing, 2018), 137.

intimate. There are hundreds of books, blogs, and articles written on touch within Christian dating relationships. Most of them concern themselves with crossing lines, boundaries, and how to stay chaste until marriage. We're all talk about the assumption of no action. We assume all touch within dating relationships to be erotic, and therefore sinful, and while it's true that touch within dating relationships *is* difficult to navigate, it makes it more difficult to navigate when we don't provide a space for faithful, loving, and godly touch between a man and woman considering marriage. What the church doesn't need is another chapter on navigating difficult boundaries regarding touch within dating, but a practice of touch that preaches the gospel in even the most intimate ways.

In Matthew 26 we see Jesus reclining at the table of another Simon, this time a leper instead of a Pharisee, and he is anointed with oil by another woman. Scholars believe it to be Mary, the sister of Martha and Lazarus, and a good friend of Jesus.[10] The disciples were indignant about what they perceived to be a waste of expensive oil, thinking the sale of it would have been a better use of resources. Jesus responds, "Why are you bothering this woman? She has done a noble thing for me. You always have the poor with you, but you do not always have me. By pouring this perfume on my body, she has prepared me for burial. Truly I tell you, wherever this

---

[10] N. T Wright (2004), "Women's Service in the Church: The Biblical Basis," St John's College, Durham, September 4, http://ntwrightpage.com/Wright_Women_Service_Church.htm.

gospel is proclaimed in the whole world, what she has done will also be told in memory of her."[11]

Jesus was unconcerned about the expensive pure oil or the seeming waste of it on His head, and more concerned about the act of preparation in which she was engaging. He cared more about the intention of her heart than the particular amount or price of her offering—the same could be said for the widow who offered the mite. One woman gave away what was obviously expensive, the other gave away what was next to nothing. In both cases, Jesus praises the women because they had one thing in common: they gave with pure, worshipful, and noble intentions.

In the same way, the Lord is less concerned with the purity of our gift (virginity) or the seeming waste of it along the way (pre-marital sex) and more concerned with the intention of our hearts. This woman touched Jesus in preparation for the whole purpose of His earthly body: The son of God came in flesh, but He had yet to be crucified, buried, and resurrected. Even though Mary and Jesus would have been friends and she would know His death was imminent, there was no way she could know for sure. She had to trust the words of Jesus to be true, and with the future of His body in mind—His death and burial—she let the expensive, pure, and extravagant sacrifice seep over His head.

Though Mary's example of anointing the head of her friend Jesus was not in the context of dating, but in burial, it was a *preparatory* touch. Her contact with Jesus was in preparation for the promised, *definitive* future, and that reality can

---

[11] Matthew 26:10–13.

comfort the hearts and minds of dating couples who desire to honor God with their bodies in a season of preparation for marriage that is neither guaranteed or promised. Our particular touch might be different than Mary's in terms of the details, but the truth is, when we touch another's body, it should always be preparatory. The person we're touching today has a future and we have to bear that in mind. We may or may not be a part of that future, but they will carry *how* we touch them today into their future. True love, pure love, the kind of love God has for us and we ought to have for one another, doesn't wait to touch. No. We touch one another with humility, purity, and faithfulness to the future we *know*—not the one we simply desire in the heat of the moment. Mary shows us the way.

Don't be confused—I am not saying there was a sexual relationship between Mary and Jesus, or even inferring it. Scripture does not teach this in any way. However, if marriage is ultimately a picture of the gospel, and union with Christ not as His earthly wife, but as part of the universal bride—the church—was Mary's future, then her example of touching Jesus can teach those along the path toward marriage. There are four characteristics of touch we can learn from her.

Friendship

Mary and Jesus were friends. Their primary relationship was that of teacher and follower, but second, they were friends. Jesus was a regular visitor in her family home, at their table, and wept at the death of Mary's brother Lazarus. There was an understanding of friendship between the two akin to that of John the Beloved. She knew she was loved by Jesus and He clearly loved her and her family. Their friendship was not a secret from others or private from the prying eyes of those who might judge the friendship between a Rabbi and a woman.

Not only does Christ call us His friends, He calls us to be friends with one another. The foundation of any dating relationship should not be sexual attraction, but love of neighbor. If it's necessary, we should be able to love any potential spouse sacrificially apart from sexual touch (though this doesn't mean the relationship will be void of all supportive or ministerial touch). Unlike what one youth pastor when I was in middle school said, sex is not the glue that holds a marriage together, friendship is. Can we, in seasons where sex is not happening for various legitimate reasons, remain friends? Can we be for one another's good, serve one another, care for one another, and remain chaste for one another when sex isn't an option?

Most touch within marriages should be the touch of friendship—not foreplay or sexual in nature (more on that in the next chapter). We should touch one another as fellow image bearers and brothers and sisters, in familial ways. Within dating and engagement, where marriage is not yet a certainty (even if there's a ring on the finger and a wedding date on the calendar), our primary relationship in biblical terms is one of family friends. Not even merely or only of friendship, but especially and particularly of friendship. This is where we will learn to care for one another's soul and mind, as well as their body without sex as a guarantee.

Because of Christ's friendship with His bride, the church—you and me, if we're children of God, we can trust Him in our friendship within a dating relationship. He shows us friendship between two distinct people, Christ and His bride, a man and a woman, is not only possible, but a beautiful illustration of the gospel.

Intimate

Mary touched the head of Jesus as He reclined. There was intimacy in their touch without it being sexual. A foundation of friendship between Mary and Jesus shows us it is possible for men and women to be simultaneously friends and to be intimate with their touch *without sin*.

Because our culture is so over-sexualized, we find it hard to believe there can be intimacy without sexuality. We actually equate intimacy with sexuality. We assume sexual intentions of intimate encounters. But the example of Mary and Jesus says otherwise. It shows us it is possible to be at rest and peace with one another, relaxed, and to experience intimate actions within that space without sin. Sin is taking what is not ours to take and sex before marriage *is* sin, and intimate touch before marriage with the express purpose of biologically preparing our bodies for sex *is* sin. But there is a kind of intimacy that does not prepare our bodies for sex, and Mary shows us its possibility. The same could be said for John when he leaned back on Jesus while they were talking. The action revealed an intimacy in friendship that had nothing to do with sexual chemistry.

Touching the head of another person feels extremely intimate, but I wonder if it's because it is simply uncommon. Or because we attribute eroticism to what should be seen as pure. Aimee Byrd's words help expand our understanding of purity: "Understanding purity is essential to relational growth. But much current teaching in the church actually prohibits relationship growth. Purity isn't merely abstention. It isn't practiced by avoidance. Purity isn't just a physical status for a virgin, nor is it even the success of a faithful marriage. Purity is preeminently about our communion with God—a foundation that flows into our other relationships."[12] If purity is the essence of our communion with God, then we will be enabled to walk not with white-knuckled avoidance, but pure-hearted intimacy. The church (and couples dating within it for that matter) has the opportunity to be like Mary in the way she touches others—both pure and intimate at the same time.

Costly

Mary's sacrifice, the oil itself, was precious and expensive. The disciples balked: "Why this waste? For this could have been sold for a large sum and given to the poor." Jesus knew the oil was costly yet didn't see her sacrifice as a waste and He doesn't see the costly sacrificial act of intimate friendship in dating as a waste either.

---

[12] Aimee Byrd, *Why Can't We Be Friends* (Phillipsburg, NJ: P&R Publishing, 2018), 69.

Not only was the oil Mary poured on the head of Jesus "very expensive," the flask from which it was poured was made of alabaster. This was a costly sacrifice for Mary, and it was poured from a costly container. In both the liquid and the container that she brought, Mary was showing that Jesus was worth everything to her.

One of the reasons we struggle so much with touch within dating relationships is because we do not understand the costly tents in which we dwell, our bodies, and we do not understand the costly sacrifice it takes to exercise restraint in the wait for marriage. Paul says our "bodies are not our own, but they have been bought with the precious blood of Christ."[13]

These bodies of death have been rescued by the Savior of the world; they are more precious than any jewel or metal found on earth. We can treat them like empty cisterns or broken wells, going again and again to sinful pleasure taking, and needing new sources for pleasure day after day. Or we can treat them like alabaster flasks full and brimming over with costly intimacy. When we treat our bodies like mere receptacles for short-lived pleasure with one another in a dating relationship, we greatly undervalue the cost Christ paid for our lives. Our bodies are truly not our own, nor the ownership of the man or woman with whom we are in a relationship. They belong to Christ and anything poured out from them belongs first and foremost to Christ. This is not the kind of sacrifice a person can give without engaging their heart. Mary was not removing her heart from the possibility

---

[13] 1 Corinthians 6:20.

of pain; she was engaging her heart knowing that not all heartbreak was worth avoiding. She was, in essence, "giving her heart away," in this costly offering to Christ.

The sacrifices we make within the dating season to honor our body (and the body of the person we are dating) are costly too. It costs the experience of not awakening love before its time. It costs the experience of remaining chaste outside of marriage in submission to God's Word. It costs unfamiliarity with sex or our spouse's body when we do come to the marriage bed. It costs incredulity of others when they hear we're trying to practice the pure intimacy of a deepening friendship as we head toward marriage and not practicing the fleeting pleasure of sexual acts in the meantime. It costs the risk of engaging our heart in care for another person, knowing that we don't have divine guarantees that our relationship will turn into marriage, and that our heart might end up broken for a little while. It costs us our reputation, as the world looks at us like we're crazy for not going too far, and the legalists looking at us like we're crazy as well, for offering appropriate affection instead of staying on opposite sides of the room.

Though the world would look at us and say "What a waste!" to the years we've chosen godliness over indulgence, and the legalists might say the same to the times we've risked "giving our heart away" or attempting godly and appropriate affection, God's not wasting our dating years. He's at work within our sacrifice of not taking what we want before its time. He's at work, making us into a person for whom Jesus is worth everything. He is changing us into people whose ultimate prize is *Christ*—not marriage, not a relationship, not sex, and not virginity.

Preparatory

In answer to the disciples' complaint that Mary's sacrifice was too costly, Jesus doesn't simply dismiss their statement about the oil being sold for the poor, He goes further. "In pouring this oil on my body, she has done it to prepare me for burial." Mary poured costly oil from a costly flask onto the head of her friend in an intimate act *because she believed the promise of Christ*, not just the future she wanted to see or the immediate future she could count on.

God has not promised marriage to any one of us. Obviously, if we're in a dating relationship, its aim should be toward the goal of seeing if marriage is an option, so the assumption is we desire marriage. But that's not a guarantee. A desire for marriage doesn't mean it will come to pass. With marriage, as with all things God has not promised us, we have to walk holding loosely to our hopes. We have to walk according to the true promises of God, the things He *has* assured us in Scripture, and not according to the wishes and hopes we have for our lives, or even the assurances we think we've sensed from Him by His Spirit. We don't *know* this person will be our husband or wife until we've said "I do." Until then, they are not our husband or wife. Even after an engagement, before the covenant of marriage takes place, we still merely have the *hope* of marriage and not the promise of it.

What does it mean, then, to touch the one we're dating or engaged to in a way that is faithful to the promises of God?

It means to touch them as though they still are not fully ours because they aren't. It means to be faithful to the future we *know* and not the future we simply *want*.

Mary knew that Christ was headed for death, burial, and resurrection not because it was what she necessarily wanted to be true or knew for sure to be true, but because it had been promised by God and spoken of by the one she called Lord. Therefore, she touched Him in faithfulness to the promise, not according to her preference. She anointed His head in preparation for separation from her and the other followers so that the real promises of God could be enacted.

Within dating and engagement, there is a physical ache for one another that little can satisfy, similar to the groaning ache we have for our groom, Christ, to come back. This is a good gift from God meant to be exercised in the right time and way. This ache is not satisfied by sex before marriage. In fact, it's not even satisfied by sex *within* marriage—not fully. There will always be a measure of dissatisfaction. This is also a good gift from God. It's there to remind us that we will never be fully satisfied outside of eternity with Christ.

※ ※ ※

As it turns out, "The purity movement had a good intention, a good motivation [chastity], but its sales pitch, of using sex as the most important thing to sell abstinence, actually led people to value and to focus on the wrong thing."[14]

---

[14] Jessica Van Der Wyngaard and Joshua Harris, *I Survived I Kissed Dating Goodbye*, documentary, 2018.

Sex is merely a crumb of the appetizer to the feast God has prepared for us. Even after the best sex, we will always be wanting more. Unless we learn at some point that sex—and all sexual touch between couples—is dissatisfying in light of eternity, we will always be playing the short game. We will wander from touch to touch, or make-out session to make-out session, or orgasm to orgasm in hopes of finding one that satiates. But that moment never comes—we have to live in light of eternity, holding dearly to what has been promised and lightly to what has not. When we touch our boyfriend or girlfriend, we have to touch them with eternity in mind. They may indeed become our spouse someday, but trying to sample a feast we're promised is only satisfied in Christ will taste bitter, empty, and leave us hungry for more. It will never be enough. Mary's touch was based on the promises of God, on what was true, not on the things she wished to be true. All our touching must be based on the same.

An Achievable End

The world's rubric for touch within dating relationships can be selfish, cheap, short, with no thought for tomorrow. The church's rubric for touch within dating relationships often takes its cues from the world's belief and practice that touch is mainly erotic, and says, therefore, it should be avoided before marriage. But Mary shows us the intimacy of touching her friend, with an understanding of its costliness and motivated by a faithful preparation to God's promises.

This was no cheap, quick action, nor was it restrained. It was costly and lavish, it was sacrificial and exorbitant.

It sounds idealistic to say this kind of touch is possible within a godly dating relationship, and perhaps it is. It didn't take long after I rebuffed Nate's first attempt to kiss me for us to expend energy practicing purity in our relationship. We felt the already/not-yet-ness of our relationship. We knew we were headed for the altar and death us do part, but we knew we weren't there yet. We took great comfort in Colossians 2:16–23:

> Therefore don't let anyone judge you in regard to food and drink or in the matter of a festival or a new moon or a Sabbath day. These are a shadow of what was to come; the substance is Christ. Let no one condemn you by delight in ascetic practices and the worship of angels, claiming access to a visionary realm. Such people are inflated by empty notions of their unspiritual mind. He doesn't hold on to the head, from whom the whole body, nourished and held together by its ligaments and tendons, grows with growth from God.
>
> If you died with Christ to the elements of this world, why do you live as if you still belonged to the world? Why do you submit to regulations: "Don't handle, don't taste, don't touch"? All these regulations refer to what is destined to perish by being used up; they are human commands and doctrines. Although

they have a reputation for wisdom by promoting self-made religion, false humility, and severe treatment of the body, they are not of any value in curbing self-indulgence.

But what is of value in curbing self-indulgence for the dating couple?

So if you have been raised with Christ, seek the things above, where Christ is, seated at the right hand of God. Set your minds on things above, not only earthly things. . . . As God's chosen ones, holy and dearly loved, put on compassion, kindness, humility, gentleness, and patience, bearing with one another and forgiving one another.[15]

It is a great joy to come under submission to the words and actions of Christ, and not "elements of the world" or "human commands and doctrines." Both present a false gospel to the Christian couple. The first is a gospel of unhindered indulgence in a mere shadow of what is to come; the second is a belief that stringent avoidance of physical touch guarantees a better future. Neither encourages the Christian couple to set their minds on things above, fighting with every fiber of their being to walk in costly, faithful preparation and intimate friendship with the one with whom their heart and body longs to be.

※ ※ ※

---

[15] Colossians 3:1–2, 12–13.

It is not idealistic to say that this kind of mind-set is possible for a dating couple and how they touch one another. In fact, it is a commandment by God for all His chosen ones. We aren't exempt from compassion, kindness, humility, gentleness, patience, long-suffering, and forgiveness during the duration of our dating relationships. If anything, the expressions of these virtues within a season of dating will both prepare and point us to and for the future whether or not we end up married. Every dating relationship we enter into is preparing us for our future marriage—if not an earthly marriage, then our heavenly one with Christ our groom. And, just as our Groom's sacrifice for us was intimate, costly, and preparatory, so too can our sacrificial touch be for one another within relationships on the journey toward marriage.

It is possible to walk with a pure heart, with a mind set on Christ, and to touch our brother or sister in a dating relationship purely and faithfully. We may have our hearts broken in beautifully humanizing ways during the process. We have an example in Mary, who shows pure touch is possible, and giving our hearts away can be a good thing if we are doing so in the sacrificial and holy way of God. She offers an example that this kind of posture is the one every Christian adopts in our long wait for our Groom to come and take us home with him.

Dr. Russell Moore writes in his book *Tempted and Tried*, "Don't let your urges scare you. Let them instead drive you to pray for the wisdom to see what you were created to be and to do."[16]

We are all groaning for the consummation of all things, the new and better earth, the sight of Christ face-to-face, the eternal feast from which we are still fasting. These groans we feel in our bodies are mere shadows of the groans we feel in our spirits. The fasting from sexual touch that we practice in dating relationships shows us in a potent way that as long as we're on earth, we're fasting from something much greater: eternal communion, intimacy, and life with Christ. The hunger pangs we feel on earth are teaching us there's a better wedding for which we wait, a better Spouse, and a better feast. Instead of ignoring those pangs when they come in dating relationships, remember what they're there to remind us of: a *better* union, the best one, the one in which there is no earthly comparison. God has promised this; it's coming for us. It was costly for Christ to give His heart, His life, away and it is costly for us too. But, I promise you, our wedding day is coming.

---

[16] Russell Moore, *Tempted and Tried* (Wheaton, IL: Crossway Publishing, 2011), 74.

CHAPTER EIGHT

Subjects and Objects
in Marriage

Though Eden is lost
Its loveliness
Remains in the heart
And the imagination.[1]
—Mary Oliver

Every heart sings a song, incomplete, until
another heart whispers back.
Those who wish to sing always find a song.
At the touch of a lover, everyone becomes a poet.[2]

---

[1] Mary Oliver, "Fireflies," *New and Selected Poems*, Volume 2 (Boston: Beacon Press, 2005), 50.
[2] Attributed to Plato, true source unknown.

I t's hot as blazes in Texas right now, forecasted to be in the 100s all next week. Last night, when the sun had gone down, I wove my way around our gardens, touching sunflowers, dahlias, pepper plants, and shaking my tomatoes gently to pollinate them. It's only the first of June and I wonder if they will survive the summer. I wonder if *I* will survive the summer. I am from the far north, a few miles from the border to Canada. Our winters up there are like the summers here in Texas, separated by more than 100 degrees, but similar in the ways we bear them, have cabin fever during them, and talk about how awful they are to strangers and friends.

It is still light at 9:00 p.m. and still hot when I lay in our bed on my side reading a library book while my husband takes his turn with our one laptop. He is writing and rewriting poetry. I am reading mystery novels. He reaches over and scratches a small circle on my back, then a wider one. I turn onto my stomach and he scratches all over my back. It is not erotic. It is not a request for sex. It is his learned way of loving me. I lay there for five minutes and feel the cells in my body respond, the oxytocin rush, the endorphins of pleasure. Again, not sexual pleasure, but the pleasure of contentment, of knowing I am loved and known and touched. This is the way I receive (and give) love most freely from those I truly love, and this is how my husband has learned to love me well.

John Keats said, "Touch has a memory,"[3] and there is memory here in the touching between those who love. This

---

[3] John Keats, "What Can I Do to Drive Away," *Complete Poems and Selected Letters of John Keats* (New York: Modern Library, a division of Random House, 2001), 361.

is why the first time you have sex with your spouse is never as fully satisfying as the one-hundredth or the thousandth. We remember the curves, the spaces, the familiar aches, the pleasures, the small signs of build-up and the crashing of release. But we also remember the specific touch of a specific person, this is also memory. Perhaps the memory is good and we feel safe there, or perhaps it was evil and we are reminded of when touch was used for ill. Either way, though, we remember.

My back is a map and the small circles my husband's hands make are showing him the way to the spot I really loved to be scratched: right between my shoulders on my upper back. This is when my pleasure is at its peak, when I feel most loved, most safe, most touched. My skin remembers him. His hands remember me. Our touch has memory.

Because touch has memory, though, marriage, which should be one of the safest places for touch, can become one of the most dangerous. We remember stolen touch, inappropriate touch, abusive touch, or unwanted touch. We also remember times when we've stolen touch from others or given it sinfully wanting something in return. All touch we've experienced before marriage informs how we touch within marriage.

The Meanings of Touch

I first heard the phrase "white-knuckle it" a few weeks after coming to my new church in Texas in 2009 and it was only then that I was able to see my own white knuckles. I'd been gripping so hard for so long onto that which I thought would earn me righteousness before God that my muscles were atrophied in position. The Lord spent the next few months peeling back my fingers from my own rigid performance mentality, and lifting my eyes to behold my God. The phrase describes a tenacious and dangerous species of self-control more about the self than about the Spirit who lives within us. We, like the Galatians, tend to believe that though our faith was begun in the Spirit, it must be finished in the flesh.[4]

While it is singleness where the phrase "white-knuckling it" is spoken most often in my circles, referring to abstention of sex, masturbation, or fantasy, I've noticed the effects of it in marriage too. Or at least the pervasive belief that, having practiced a form of purity through white-knuckling before marriage, one can come to marriage without restraint. Permitted sex? Yes, please! All the time! Every day! It only takes a few weeks or, for some, only one night, for us to realize self-control regarding sex has just as present a role in marriage as it does in singleness, perhaps more, as "the two will become one flesh."[5] One plus one equals twice the complications.

When I entered into marriage, as I said in chapter 1, I brought with me the full expectation that our bodies would be given entirely to one another without restraint. I knew it would take time, I knew it would be difficult, I knew sex might hurt or be awkward or messy, but I fully expected that we would lay ourselves down for one another, literally, and

---

[4] Galatians 3:3.
[5] Mark 10:8.

figure it out. What I didn't expect was, for us, sex was easy and all other touch wasn't.

I married a hyper-sensitive person regarding touch. While my bubble of personal space ends where my skin begins, Nate's is much wider and not limited to human contact. While I'll wear an uncomfortable pair of shoes or pants for a whole day without thinking to change, he'll barely try them on before casting them to the bottom of the closet never to be seen or worn again. It took three years before I could toss his favorite pair of corduroys—three sizes too big and so threadbare you could see through the knees. He ran track for the University of Texas and has every single T-shirt from every single race he ran—all threadbare, faded, and brilliantly soft. When he has a favorite item of clothing, he wears it all the time because of how it feels to him. What I didn't realize when we got married (after a short and chaste engagement) is my body had not yet reached the comfortability factor of his favorite T-shirts. That's not to say I was worth the same as his T-shirt, but that my body was unfamiliar, my hands surprising, my shoulder against his restricting, my hugs too tight or too long. I was confused. Touch, for me, had mostly been practiced as a form of love; I was adept in its language and I wanted to use it with my husband. But it seemed that the only place my touch was welcomed regularly was leading up to sex.

It took many conversations to come to the place we are now, where Nate's touch is more frequent and my demand for it is less. I still ask for his physical warmth and comfort when I am feeling particularly in need of it, but he offers it before I can ask most of the time.

Imago Dei and We Are Family

In those early days of marriage one of the most helpful realizations to me was the recognition that before being my husband, Nate was a human being created in the image of God and he was my brother in Christ. Before any obligation toward me as his wife, before any need, desire, or inclination toward sex, before participation in the beautiful mystery of marriage, he was a man created in the image of God and he was my sibling in the Lord.

A few months ago, during a retreat we planned for personal growth and our marriage, Nate and I asked one another what we would like to see the other learn more deeply in those four days. Tears welled up in my eyes when Nate said, "I would like you to learn that although we are one, we are also two. Fusion with me doesn't mean that you negate who you are, who God has made you to be, your gifts, inclinations, and preferences." One of the greatest struggles for me in our marriage is to not curve myself so fully to him that I forget I am God's workmanship as well. I do not idolize him or marriage, so much as I idolize peace, and disappearing into him or fusing together in marriage can often seem like the most peace-keeping way.

Part of this is in reaction to a culture of hyper-feminism that demands women be loud and in charge, full of opinions on everything and adamant about getting our way. Part of it, though, is a natural inclination toward invisibility that I have spent the whole of my life fighting. One of the most helpful things for me to remember is that just as Nate is an image bearer and my brother, I am also an image bearer and

his sister in Christ. As I fully embody that which God created me to be, to fulfill my whole intention on earth as an
equal heir and fellow workman in the kingdom, I become a
better wife than I would be if I simply sought to be a good
wife. There is no shortage of counsel in the church on how
to be a good wife, but I am not just any man's wife; I am my
husband's and he is mine and we are God's, together and
as individuals. My chief identity is not "wife." Nate's is not
"husband." Our chief identity is "son" and "daughter" of the
Most High and children in the family of God.

Touch in marriage becomes complicated when see ourselves and the other as primarily a husband or primarily a
wife, and sex as the primary act of marriage that sets us apart
from others. If we only view ourselves as there to partner with
or please the other, we will forget there is a higher calling
than being a husband or a wife. No wonder there's so much
confusion around the role of marriage in the church and society today—the burden we place on it and on its participants
is far too heavy to bear.

How do we exercise submission to our bodies and to an
expression of touch within marriage when sex is seen as so
crucial to the health of a marriage? Put another way: how do
we healthily touch our spouse in submission to our own bodies and in service to theirs?

Unsurprisingly, Jesus shows us a way.

Authority and Submission

Chapter 13 of John, the narrative of Jesus washing the feet of His disciples, opens with these words:

> Before the Passover Festival, Jesus knew that his hour had come to depart from this world to the Father. Having loved his own who were in the world, he loved them to the end.
>
> Now when it was time for supper, the devil had already put it into the heart of Judas, Simon Iscariot's son, to betray him. Jesus knew that the Father had given everything into his hands, that he had come from God, and that he was going back to God. So he got up from supper, laid aside his outer clothing, took a towel, and tied it around himself. Next, he poured water into a basin and began to wash his disciples' feet and to dry them with the towel tied around him.[6]

There is so much in this passage for the Christian, namely the orderliness to the Father's intention for Christ. Christ, at the right time, having done exactly what He was purposed to do, to its very completion, prepared to leave the world. In the midst of His own preparation, He stripped himself of His garments, became like a servant, died to Himself, and cleaned the grime from the feet of His disciples. Paul said it like this to the church at Philippi: "who, existing in the form

---

[6] John 13:1–5.

of God, did not consider equality with God as something to be exploited. Instead he emptied himself by assuming the form of a servant, taking on the likeness of humanity. And when he had come as a man, he humbled himself by becoming obedient to the point of death—even to death on a cross."[7]

Kathy Keller in *The Meaning of Marriage*, writes about Jesus washing the disciples' feet, saying, "In Jesus we see all the authoritarianism of authority laid to rest, and all the humility of submission glorified."[8] In making Himself vulnerable and serving His disciples by washing the filth from their feet, He was, of many things, foreshadowing His act to come—the ultimate sacrifice He'd be making on their behalf, the ultimate cleaning of their bodies and souls, the ultimate act of authority and submission simultaneously, which is of course His death, burial, and resurrection. Put simply: Jesus was obedient to God, living out exactly who He was. He had full authority and with that authority He laid His life down in full submission to His body's purpose and intention: the sacrificial lamb of God come to take away the sins of the world.

A reason touch within marriage is so rife with complication is because we misread our ultimate purpose as humans and therefore misuse our bodies in moving toward it. If we think sex is the pinnacle (or even if we simply act like it is by giving it more credence and weight than it actually holds) and act like it's the goal within marriage, all touch will be

---

[7] Philippians 2:6–8.
[8] Tim and Kathy Keller, *The Meaning of Marriage* (New York: Dutton, a Penguin Group, 2011), 178.

problematic. C. S. Lewis, in his oft-quoted passage from his sermon, *The Weight of Glory*, says, "It would seem that Our Lord finds our desires not too strong, but too weak. We are half-hearted creatures, fooling about with drink and sex and ambition when infinite joy is offered us, like an ignorant child who wants to go on making mud pies in a slum because he cannot imagine what is meant by the offer of a holiday at the sea. We are far too easily pleased."[9]

Our problem is that when we aren't submitting our bodies and their desires to God's ultimate design for them, we end up settling for sex—even married sex—thinking it's the best thing we can get on earth. But while our infinite joy may have to wait until eternity, our abundant life begins now and sex can't be the mark or measure of what abundant life looks like for the Christian. Abundant life for the Christian begins when we learn to lay our life down. Unfortunately, in marriage we often misuse our authority (and bodily autonomy) in order to assert authority over the other instead of laying our lives down.

Jesus doesn't act this way with His own Bride. With the church, instead of misusing His authority, He laid aside all the clout of the royalty He was due as the Son of God, took on the form of a servant, washed the feet of His followers, and showed them the way forward was not the way of an earthly king but a heavenly submissive one. He submitted to the order of His Father both in time and in action. He handled grime-covered, calloused feet that had walked through animal excrement, on dusty roads, and among unclean people,

[9] C. S. Lewis, *The Weight of Glory* (New York: Harper Collins, 1976), 26.

and washed them clean. He was saying, "Whoever would be great among you must be your servant, and whoever would be first among you must be your slave, even as the Son of Man came not to be served but to serve, and to give his life as a ransom for many."[10]

When we come to marriage as if we're kings and queens, believing we are owed an experience of touch according to our preferences, we are acting against the example of Christ. Whether it is something as simple as holding hands and engaged back-rubs or something as complicated as sex, we are not *owed* touch. We are to give it, yes, but give it expecting nothing in return. This is a hard truth for the married person. Especially if they've white-knuckled their way to marriage, hoping for a whopping return on their investment of chastity before marriage. And perhaps even more if they've had a negative experience of touch before marriage and it informs how they give or receive or withhold it within marriage. Paul Tripp writes,

> Love isn't about placing people in our debt
> and waiting for them to pay off their debts.
> Love isn't a negotiation for mutual good. Real
> love does not demand reciprocation, because
> real love isn't motivated by the return on
> investment. No, real love is motivated by the
> good that will result in the life of the person
> being loved.[11]

---

[10] Matthew 20:26–28 (ESV).

[11] Paul Tripp, *What Did You Expect?* (Wheaton, IL: Crossway Publishing, 2010), 189.

If we come to marriage thinking it will be the place where all our sexual needs are met, but where we will not need to lay down our authority, autonomy, and even our history, and submit to joyful service of the other, marriage will be a miserable place for us. But if we can come to marriage like Christ came to His disciples, laying aside any entitlement we have and washing their most painful, disgusting, world-trodden places without expecting anything in return, this is the image-bearing and familial nature of marriage. This is where we are simply humans before one another and not objects for sex or pleasure. Ragan Sutterfield learned this shortly after marriage after a lifetime of mistreating his body through crash diets, promiscuous sex, and no exercise, "Now, under the influence of Emily's love, I was living into my body as subject rather than object."[12] He was learning what it meant to be a subject of a heavenly kingdom instead of an object of his own worship.

Subjects of a Kingdom, Not Objects for Worships

What does it mean to live as subjects of the kingdom within marriage regarding touch? Let's consider some typical marriage stories we all hear some version of in the church.

Marriage 1

In the first marriage, the man and the woman grew up in stable Christian environments, perhaps attended private

---

[12] Tim and Kathy Keller, *The Meaning of Marriage* (New York: Dutton, a Penguin Group, 2011), 179.

school and Christian universities. He dreamed of being in ministry, she always dreamed of being a wife and mother. They both came to marriage virgins. She has perfected the art of saying "No" to boys since she was in high school and prides herself on coming to her marriage bed pure—she practiced a form of self-control. He hid his secret sin of pornography use and habitual masturbation since high school, while maintaining a shiny exterior of the "good gospel guy." He keeps white-knuckling his sin and failing occasionally, and she keeps saying "No" until their honeymoon when his interior desires come out in full force and her perfected art of no suddenly has to turn to an immediate and unfamiliar yes.

Touch, for them, feels odd and even dangerous—any form of it. She only knows how not to be touched, comfortable with both withholding pleasure and having pleasure withheld from herself. He only knows how to touch himself, always culminating in pleasure, never how to be patient and please his wife.

Eventually, because the wife is accustomed to saying no, she becomes a steel trap of pleasure, withholding or doling it out as she feels comfortable. Any initiation of touch from her husband is going to cause her to do the math, "Do I or don't I feel like having sex?" The husband is accustomed to the yes of immediate pleasure he had access to through masturbation before marriage, so he feels constantly withheld from—even if she says yes one out of the four times he asks. He begins to approach all touch of her timidly because he knows she's always going to interpret it as an invitation for sex, until eventually he's returned to habitual masturbation and rarely touches his wife anymore. Their lack of good, healthy touch has stemmed from their unhealthy approach to sex. They both prided themselves on self-control, but it was birthed out of a blind commitment to purity instead of submission of their bodies to their Creator. They may have said no to what they were supposed to say no to in the technical sense, but they weren't saying yes to touch in all the healthy and God-glorifying ways they should have over the years.

Marriage 2

In the next marriage, the man and the woman did not grow up in Christian environments, they both went to secular universities, they both had sex for the first time in high school or college, and they continued to have multiple sexual partners until they met one another in their late twenties shortly after getting saved. They were committed to a life of purity after becoming believers, but they were both so accustomed to falling into sex quickly that living chaste lives felt nearly impossible while they were dating. They also began to have accompanying guilt every single time they had sex or came close to it. They cannot have any kind of intimacy without a nagging sense of guilt and shame. Once married, they interpret any of kind touch as an invitation to sex—as it was in their single days—and therefore cannot bear being touched or touching at a time when sex isn't convenient. Touch becomes something that only occurs when sex is convenient; otherwise it's shoved off or ignored. Sex is seen as the reward. Touch is dangerous for them too.

They are both accustomed to saying yes to sex whenever initiated, but the incessant guilt from their sexual indiscretions before marriage keeps hanging around. They feel like they cannot shed the shame or the past mental images that inevitably accompanies sex. They can stuff it away or pretend it doesn't exist, but sex, for them, is tainted by guilt they haven't dealt with before the cross of Christ. They don't want to feel shame, so they avoid sex, and therefore avoid any healthy touch because of what it has historically led to.

Marriage 3

In the third marriage, both husband and wife became believers in their twenties. He had multiple sexual partners before becoming a believer; she had none. He had struggled with pornography and habitual masturbation before submitting his life to Christ. Upon conversion and some discipleship, he began to see the fruitlessness of these habits, and the damage they could do to a marriage. She made out with boyfriends and experimented with masturbation a few times, but knew ultimately this wasn't going to bring the kind of joy she knew possible in marriage.

They both sought the grace of God for their sin and continued in pursuit of Him, praying for an overflow of purity in their lives. They came to marriage with a healthy understanding of sex and of their own inadequacies. He knew he had to prefer her needs, desires, and pleasure above his own. She knew the same about him. Sex became a journey for them, imperfect and clumsy at first, both learning one another's bodies and both learning to voice their preferences, but it was never dangerous. It was safe. And therefore, touch in their marriage was safe. Touch was not an invitation to sex as much as an assurance that the other was there, seeing, knowing, and loving.

Here, sex is seen rightly: where sin did abound, grace abounded more. Touch, for them, doesn't automatically signal sex is around the corner, and sex, when it occurs, is pleasurable because it is about the other and not the self. What's striking about this marriage is they submitted themselves to the created order for their bodies, they submitted the struggle of their urges and actions to the grace of God and the help of the Spirit, and within marriage, they submitted their bodies to one another in honor and love. They know their purpose, they know their sin, and they know their Savior, and this changes everything for them. Sex isn't seen as a prize, a guarantee, a fix, or merely a method of getting love, respect, or pleasure. It is in its proper place in their marriage, and therefore all their touch is seen as right, good, and healthy. This right relationship with sex enables them to make themselves vulnerable and serve one another through other non-sexual touch.

A Way Forward

There is a way forward for Marriage 1 and Marriage 2. They can look to Christ. For just as Christ submitted His body to serve His disciples' bodies, and eventually submitted His body to death on a cross, they (and we all) have been set free to do the same. The Kellers again: "Both women and men get to 'play the Jesus role' in marriage—Jesus in his sacrificial authority, Jesus in his sacrificial submission."[13] And that's the hope for these marriages, and all Christian marriages. Both parties get to be Christlike, and when they are, touch works.

Christ lived and served in the body He had (and has) on the earth He inhabited. His love, in the words of my favorite poem, called Him "to the things of this world."[14] Washing filthy feet wasn't below Him, it was part of what He came to do. He knew in order to set His people free to set their affections on the coming kingdom instead of "fooling about with drink and sex and ambition when infinite joy is offered,"[15] He would have to teach them to care for the things of this world *in their proper place and proper way*. He would have to teach them to touch, clean, care for, and nourish their earthly bodies. In marriage this sort of heart-posture, not sex, is our great calling. We must make ourselves like servants,[16] not kings, discarding anything we use as covering or for self-protection.

---

[13] Ibid.

[14] Richard Wilbur, "Love Calls Us to the Things of This World," *New and Collected Poems* (Orlando: Harcourt Brace Jovanovich, 1989), 233.

[15] C. S. Lewis, *The Weight of Glory* (New York: Harper Collins, 1976), 26.

[16] Making ourselves like "servants" in our marriages does not mean making ourselves what the world might consider a sexual servant or one in abusive sexual servitude to a spouse. *Servant* here is a nod to the posture and heart of Christ—that He was willing to take care of or "serve" our needs. On the heart level and the action level, He was the ultimate servant, though He didn't have to be, and we should be likewise in our touch and in all our actions with others as believers. This does not mean being a pushover, a doormat, or a sexual slave. It means considering another as more important than yourself, along with your spouse who is doing the

For the one who prided herself on her purity before marriage, she needs to ask herself, "Who is the most pure and who protects my purity?" The answer to that is God. God is most pure, and any purity we have in us is both a reflection of and a gift from God. It is His purity, not ours, that we walk in. Who is the keeper of her purity then? God, not her. Every day she remains pure in body, mind, and spirit, is a gift from God, not by any work or white-knuckling of her own. Her purity is not her gift to her husband on her wedding night; it is merely the grace of God at work in her life sustaining her virginity. Therefore, she can give of her body not only in sex, but in all sorts of service to her husband as an act of worship to God, not worship of herself. (The same mind-set should be true of him for her sake as well.)

For the one who engaged in masturbation, pornography, or habitual sexual activity before marriage, they need to ask themselves, "Who gives the most pleasure and why do I seek a lesser substitute?" The answer again is God. God is the giver of our pleasure, and short-lived indulgences that we seek from this world instead of Him are no pleasure at all—not really. They might bring a rush of pleasure but it's gone within seconds, which then only begins the chase for another, and usually more deviant, thrill. This is not the "pleasures of God are forevermore," of which the Psalms speak. One who knows they are bearing the image of God knows the pleasures available to them in submitting their desires to the Lord are profoundly better. The joy He offers is longer lasting.

---

same for you. The connotation here is "outdoing the other in honor and consideration," not sexual servitude.

The comfort He offers is more eternal. The fidelity He gives is more faithful. The intimacy He offers is deeper than any earthly spouse can give.

For the one who prided herself on purity, again, who views her new husband as one who is only interested in sex, pleasure, and satisfaction, and who cannot view his normal touch as anything other than an invitation, she needs to remember he may be incorrectly interpreting his *desire* for pleasure as a *need* for pleasure, but she also needs to remember he was indeed made, among many things, for pleasure (and so was she). He was made to be pleased primarily by God, but also by the gifts of God. God knew it was not good for man to be alone and gave him a wife to be a helper and friend to him. A wife who can interpret her husband's desire to be with her (both intimately and in every other way) as a good and God-given desire for oneness and love and connection is a gift.

For the husband who feels like his wife is sexually withholding from him, he needs to remember she is an image bearer of God, made to be pleased by the gifts of God, yes, but ultimately, by God Himself. He cannot demand she find that pleasure ultimately in him. He needs to understand her quest for purity (even if it was misguided in some ways) or her history of being sinfully touched has probably convinced her to view sex as a dirty thing or at the very least an unnecessary thing. His job is to walk in humility, patience, and long-suffering. To woo her with his love, just as God does for us. He cannot be a trap she tries to avoid, but a haven she runs toward. A husband who serves his wife faithfully—even when sex isn't on the table—is a gift.

When two spouses view one another primarily as fellow subjects in the kingdom of God (and not as objects to be worshipped), they begin to rightly order their desires and preferences. Sex becomes a gift instead of something we're owed, and therefore, all our touch toward one another is not charged with sexuality as much as it is full of love.

Lewis again says,

> Sexual desire, without Eros, wants *it*, the *thing in itself*; Eros wants the Beloved. The *thing* is a sensory pleasure; that is, an event occurring within one's own body. We use a most unfortunate idiom when we say, of a lustful man prowling the streets, that he 'wants a woman.' Strictly speaking, a woman is just what he does not want. He wants a pleasure for which a woman happens to be the necessary piece of apparatus. How much he cares about the woman as such may be gauged by his attitude to her five minutes after fruition (one does not keep the carton after one has smoked the cigarettes).[17]

Christians, who view one another as subjects in the King's kingdom instead of objects of pleasure or worship, bypass this sort of thing altogether. When it comes to touch, they don't seek merely a body, an experience, a release, or an

---

[17] C. S. Lewis, *The Four Loves* (New York: Harper One, 2017), 94.

"apparatus," as Lewis says, but instead, they seek a *person*. In this way, viewing one's spouse as God's subject instead of your own plaything is the difference between objectifying a person and humanizing them.

When we're able to distinguish merely sexual touch from loving touch, we're freed up to serve as Christ served His disciples. The Image of the Invisible God[18] is serving those who bear the image of God, the One who was unashamed of calling us brothers and sisters,[19] washing the feet of His siblings.

Love, Jesus Himself, called to the things of this world, has called us to love the people of this world as He loved them. Love embodied means we should touch our husband or wife as if they are imprinted with the very image of God, as if their bodies really do matter infinitely more than mere objects for sex, as if they should be considered family who deserve respect, love, care, and nourishment. Because the truth is, they are and they do and they should.

---

[18] Colossians 1:15.
[19] Hebrews 2:11.

CHAPTER NINE

Let the Little Children Come

It is easier to build strong children
than to repair broken men.[1]
—Frederick Douglass

Feel guilty falling asleep while praying?
How do you feel when a child nods off in your
lap? And how much more must your Heavenly
Father feel about you when this happens?
There. Feel better? You should![2]
—Scott Sauls

---

[1] Written in 1855 in dialogs Frederick Douglass had with white slave-owners.
[2] Scott Sauls, Twitter Post. April 8, 2018, 10:45 a.m., https://twitter.com/scottsauls/status/982992761799499777.

W e have a family joke. It's that more wooden spoons were broken over my behind than any of the other seven of my siblings combined. It's only partially true, though, because I remember a few instances of broken spoons over my knuckles, too. In one instance in particular, the spoon splintered so comically that I laughed and my mother hit harder, the skin of my hand pinching between the split bowl of the spoon.

The last time I remember being spanked, it was by the belt, and what I remember most of all was the snap the belt made as my dad held it in his hands while I walked into my parents' bedroom. I cannot recall my wrongdoing, but I do know it was the last time I bent over his knees. I was fifteen. It was around this time that I realized if I held back my words and sharp wit, nobody would notice me, belts included. Invisibility became my shield.

We were a robustly demonstrative family—everything was the loudest or the best or the worst or taken to the nth degree. In hindsight, my memory of our childhood home is probably more colored by my own aversion to loudness or chaos or a lack of peace than absolute truth, but there was a roughness to our home that anyone could see. It was dominated by testosterone, the male anatomy, dirt, skinned knees, broken bones, and too many failed tree houses to count. It was also dominated by domination. Who was the biggest and strongest and had the best argument? They were the winner. This was one of the reasons my mouth got me into so much trouble. I wasn't bigger or stronger, but I was wittier. My tongue was quick and while I might disagree with some of the discipline methods used in our home, I can't imagine having to live with a ten- or twelve-year-old me. God bless my parents and my brothers.

At some point, I learned to rein in my tongue and figured out that my verbal aptitude was better suited to writing. To my knowledge, another wooden spoon was never broken in our house again.

Foolishness in the Hearts of Children

The sin of anger wasn't dead in my heart, though; it was only dormant. A few years later it flared in one white-hot moment I will never forget.

Our younger brother Andrew was fourteen when he died in a sudden accident. And though the family dog was the family's, we all knew he was Andrew's. I have a dog now—Harper Nelle—and marvel at how an animal can imprint itself so wholly on their human. In all her Soft-Coated Wheaten Terrier glory, she lays on the bathroom floor while I shower, sleeps at the crook of my knees at night, is anxious when I am gone more than a day and, I confess, I feel anxious away from her too. This was the kind of dog our golden retriever Alex was to our brother Andrew. He followed Andrew around our small homestead, into the barn for chores, sleeping by his bed at night. They were inseparable. One of my favorite photos of Andrew is of him and Alex sitting on the top step of the white front porch of our farmhouse. Andrew's broad smile and gapped teeth and wide-set eyes all grinning together in perfect unison. A friend of ours once described our family's uniform smile as "more in the eyes than the mouth." It is easy to memorialize the dead in superlatives we can no longer prove, but I think this smile was truer of Andrew than any of us. And he was never more happy than with his dog.

When I was nineteen, a few months after Andrew died, my seventeen-year-old brother, Danny, and I were in an argument over who had won the loyalty of our grieving dog. I think now it was more about who was grieving the loss of our younger brother more. Danny said the words, "*My* dog," and an anger unlike any I've experienced before or since flared in me. I lifted my hand and slapped him hard across the face. We both stood there stunned, the white mark on his face turning a fuming red. I sputtered, "I'm sorry. I'm so sorry." He stood taller than me, his chest puffed out for one hostile minute, his face reddening more, and then, as if he knew his strength would crush me, he turned and ran.

I do not remember if we resolved this, or if we resolved whose dog Alex became.

When I think of the moments where I am most ashamed of a physical action, this slap comes to mind. It was a moment in which several things occurred at once. I was angry. I used my body sinfully in response. I harmed one I loved. I was immediately sorry. But it didn't change anything. No apology could change the fact that I had harmed one I loved in anger.

Scorekeeping Bodies

In the past few years, as I've begun to understand the far-reaching effects of trauma on our bodies, I've simultaneously begun to accept God's grace for that wayward slap. The point is: it wasn't wayward. It wasn't an anomaly. It was a physical response to an impossible situation in which both my brother and I were traumatized by the loss of our brother. Andrew's death felt meaningless and intangible. He was there, robust, tall, full of life on a rainy April morning at 9:00 a.m. and then he just wasn't on the same rainy April morning at 9:07 a.m., his misshapen body lying in the middle of wet, black pavement just to the left of the yellow dotted lines. There is nothing to hold onto in the aftermath of a grief and instability like that; I suppose you have to touch what you can. I think, in hindsight—and not at all to excuse my sin of harming my brother—what I really wanted was to care about something real. Danny. The dog. I wanted to solidify something that was anything but firm and sure. I was touching what I could (albeit sinfully), and in that moment, it was the cheek of my other still-living brother.

Bessel Van Der Kolk talks about this. He mentioned once that simple and foundational things that our bodies always do—things like eating and releasing toxins and using the bathroom—are all things that "go wrong when you get traumatized. The most elementary bodily functions go awry when you are terrified. So trauma treatment starts at the foundation of a body that can sleep, a body that can rest, a body that feels safe, a body that can move."[3] In the wake of trauma, our bodies misfire, mis-function, and mis-move.

---

[3] Krista Tippett, "Bessel van der Kolk, How Trauma Lodges in the Body," *On Being with Krista Tippett*, March 9, 2017, https://onbeing.org/programs /bessel-van-der-kolk-how-trauma-lodges-in-the-body-mar2017/.

Over the years, I've come to see that the slap my body reflexively generated was a moment of both great sin and great
suffering happening at the same time.

It makes me think about all the ways we have used our
bodies for harm toward ourselves and others, unknowingly
or unthinkingly because of the ways we have been harmed
by others or by circumstances beyond our control. Wounded
people wound people, as they say. Take my parents, for example, and their disciplinary measures. How much of the way in
which I was spanked or the frequency of the spankings or the
harshness of them was less about my fiery tongue, and more
about their own histories—the ways they were disciplined or
punished, the mistreatments they'd experienced, their fears
and doubts and hurts about themselves or their children?
I have often thought of the many times I flung the words,
"You hate me!" or "I hate you!" at my mother and she felt her
only recourse was to discipline me physically. How hurt she
must have been by the words of her only daughter and how,
perhaps, it might have seemed the only defense she had was
to hurt back.

All our lives tell a complex story. Every experience is formative for us, and every part anyone has played in our lives
affects, on some level, how we live, move, and breathe. We
are awkward with our bodies or free with them or restrained
with them or liberal with them in part because of the sum of
our experiences. And all of our experiences, at the very least
and earliest, start with our family. This is where we learn to
walk and to fall and to get back up and sometimes to not.
From our very first breath, as we came squalling out of the

womb and into the hands of a doctor and then laid on the chest of our mother or whisked away to an incubator, our experiences of touch are being formed. As Margaret Atwood would say, "Touch comes before sight, before speech. It is the first language and the last, and it always tells the truth."[4]

A friend of mine adopted a few years ago and she, her husband, and near-toddler boy spent a few days with us recently. She was recounting how when the boy was born, she removed her shirt and tucked him in there, next to her skin. Security for him was directly related to skin-to-skin care. In order to thrive and to develop into a growing child, he needed to be touched.

Rob Moll tells us why:

> When doctors encouraged new mothers to hold their infants, skin to skin, for an hour soon after birth and then for five more hours over the next three days, they found that those mothers were vastly more attuned to their babies. The results even five years later are astonishing. A total of just six hours of skin to skin contact in the first three days resulted in mothers who spent more time soothing their babies, caressing them and making eye contact a full month later. One year later, those mothers were found to ask the doctor more questions during an annual checkup.

---

[4] Margaret Atwood, *The Blind Assassin* (New York: Random House, 2000), 256.

They also helped the doctor more. Two years later, they need to give their children fewer commands than mothers who hadn't spent that extra time cuddling their babies. Perhaps more shocking is that five years after those six hours of physical contact, those children scored higher on IQ and language tests.[5]

Our bodies learn to function in the world from the very first seconds of life outside the womb, and they never stop gathering information about how to engage with the world until our death. They do it innately, without thought, and especially in infancy and childhood. We reflect with our hands the way others' use their hands with us. The body of my father using his hands to slap the belt against itself as I walked into my parents' bedroom was informed by his father, and his father's use of the switch was informed by his father, and his father, and his father, and so on. Our bodies, as Van Der Kolk said, "keep the score"—whether we're aware of it or not, they're carrying with them the wounds and scars and anomalies and genetic makeup of generations past.

This sounds like victimization—as though we are incapable of seeking grace from God and receiving it in such a way that we are changed moving forward. But it isn't considered victimization to diagnose a family medical history of heart disease, for example, and to receive the common grace of God through medicine, supplements, exercise techniques,

---

[5] Rob Moll, *What Your Body Knows about God* (Downers Grove, IL: InterVarsity Press, 2014), 40.

and other helps. So why would we consider taking stock of our mental and emotional history as playing the victim? We all, as I said in chapter 3, suffer from an issue of blood—not just the bloodline of our own story, but the bloodline of all humanity that began at the Fall: sin.

We are what Paul called "clay jars" in 2 Corinthians 4 and we "carry the death of Jesus in our body." Why? "So that the life of Jesus may also be displayed in our body." Here's the passage in context:

> Now we have this treasure in clay jars, so that this extraordinary power may be from God and not from us. We are afflicted in every way but not crushed; we are perplexed but not in despair; we are persecuted but not abandoned; we are struck down but not destroyed. We always carry the death of Jesus in our body, so that the life of Jesus may also be displayed in our body. For we who live are always being given over to death for Jesus's sake, so that Jesus's life may also be displayed in our mortal flesh. So then, death is at work in us, but life in you. And since we have the same spirit of faith in keeping with what is written, I believed, therefore I spoke, we also believe, and therefore speak. For we know that the one who raised the Lord Jesus will also raise us with Jesus and present us with you. Indeed, everything is for your benefit so that, as grace extends through more and more

people, it may cause thanksgiving to increase
to the glory of God.

Therefore we do not give up. Even though
our outer person is being destroyed, our inner
person is being renewed day by day. For our
momentary light affliction is producing for us
an absolutely incomparable eternal weight of
glory. So we do not focus on what is seen, but
on what is unseen. For what is seen is temporary, but what is unseen is eternal.[6]

Though this passage refers to all the situations in which
Paul's preaching of the gospel was suppressed (whether by
direct attack from Paul's opponents, storms, shipwrecks,
beatings, and so on), its principles still apply to the many
of us who have been afflicted, perplexed, persecuted, struck
down in the context of family. Our bodies have *felt* crushed,
in despair, abandoned, and destroyed. But Paul says they
are not. The life of Jesus is displayed even in this mortal
flesh. And even though this outer person, this body, is being
destroyed even as I write and you read, our inner person
is being renewed day by day. God is at work even in these
broken bodies and broken bloodlines, these physical and
emotional histories marred by brokenness. Our bodies will
keep score of our histories and act out in many ways. But God
keeps a better score—the score of the gospel of Jesus Christ,
which is a perfect one. And God acted out in a stronger and
better way than we ever could—He acted on our behalf by

---

[6] 2 Corinthians 4:7–18.

paying for all those broken places and bloodlines, and healing them both now and in the full resurrection to come.

As It Seemed Best

A few years ago I heard a sermon called "The Father Wound." I wept through the whole sermon, and it marks a moment of freedom for me in regard to the way I was parented. The pastor said,

> Have you ever thought for a moment that maybe your dad wasn't as malicious as you think he is? It's interesting, in Hebrews, chapter 12, verses 9–10, it says, "Besides this, we have had earthly fathers who disciplined us and we respected them. Shall we not much more be subject to the Father of spirits and live? For they [your dads] disciplined us for a short time as it seemed best to them, but he [God] disciplines us for our good, that we may share his holiness."
>
> There's an interesting cryptic little phrase in there that never made sense to me before, but I understand it now. Your dad parented you *as seemed best to him*. Maybe the possibility is that your dad was just simply dealing with his own wounds, his own pain. It doesn't excuse him, but maybe it helps explain a little better that maybe your dad didn't wake up in the morning and simply think to himself,

How can I really screw up my kid's life this morning? How can I just cripple them in such an amazing way that they'll hate me for the rest of their life? Let's figure this out. Do you really think your dad did that? I would bet most dads didn't. I don't think my dad did.[7]

This realization was stunning to me: "as it seemed best to him." I saw, in that moment, how so much of how I was handled by my family and how I handled them, was wrapped up in simply doing what seemed best to us in the moment. All the broken moments and all the best ones—we were all doing what seemed best to us in that moment with the information we had and the skills we had and the assumptions we made and the futures we were unsure of. We did what seemed best or fitting or right—even if it was irrevocably harmful or sinful. As the Proverbs would say, we were all doing—we are all still doing—simply what "seems right to a person."[8]

In Mark 10, we see the disciples behaving similarly:

People were bringing little children to him in order that he might touch them, but the disciples rebuked them. When Jesus saw it, he was indignant and said to them, "Let the little children come to me. Don't stop them, because the kingdom of God belongs to such

---

[7] Shea Sumlin, "The Father Wound," sermon preached at The Village Church, Flower Mound, August 2012, https://www.tvcresources.net/resource-library/sermons/the-father-wound-flower-mound.
[8] Proverbs 14:12; 16:25.

as these. Truly I tell you, whoever does not receive the kingdom of God like a little child will never enter it." After taking them in his arms, he laid his hands on them and blessed them.[9]

In context, it's important to note that Jesus had just finished teaching on the decidedly adult topics of divorce, remarriage, and eunuchs. Immediately following this, parents brought their children to Jesus for His blessing. I like to think that the disciples, in their belief that this was adult-time-only, were like the lifeguards at Adult Swim time, blowing their whistles and telling the kids to get out of the pool. The disciples did what seemed best to them and rebuked the parents, shooing the kids away.

But Jesus.

For the whole of our lives there will be some who try to hold us back physically, spiritually, mentally, or emotionally from moving forward into the best of what Jesus has for us. They will do it because they earnestly believe they are doing what's best—not because it *is* best, but because it *seems* best. When it comes to touch, they will discipline too harshly or not at all. They will withhold touch or give it sinfully. They will be cold in response to our touch or effusively suffocating with it. And Jesus is right there in the midst of it all. In this passage, He moves into the space of what *seems* best to the disciples and says instead what *is* best: "Leave the kids alone and don't try to hold them back from Me—these are the ones

---

[9] Mark 10:13–16.

the kingdom is for!" And then He places His hands on them for a blessing.

In every family since the very first family, we have used our hands for good and evil. Adam never raised his hand in protest to stop the serpent from deceiving his wife, as far as we can tell. Eve used her hands to pull the fruit from the tree and then hand it to her husband. Their son used his hands to kill his brother. Their descendants used their hands to rape women, remove children from their home, deceive brothers, defeat giants, kill lions with their bare hands, bear gifts for an infant King, and then nail Him to a cross. Every person who has ever lived has used their hands for harm and for good, and each one has done it thinking it seemed best in the moment.

Perhaps they were blinded by a white-hot rage like I was when I slapped my brother across the face, yet the rage was born in an unspeakable grief—Jesus sees that grief and died for it. Perhaps they were blinded by generations of broken fathering or abject disappointment in their own parenting—our Father shows Himself to be a better Father. Perhaps they were merely guided by what they saw their parents doing—the Spirit is a better guide. Perhaps they were enacting out of lack, out of what they wish their parents had done—the Spirit gives a better comfort. Or perhaps they feel they have no control over their body—here, our God shows Himself to be more sovereign. Jesus cares about the little children, and the hands He lays on them are full of blessing. He inserts Himself right into the narrative of what seems best in the moment to show what *is* best, and He does so using His hands.

However you were touched or left untouched, however your parents disciplined you as it seemed best to them, however you use your hands now as it seems best to you, Jesus is beckoning to you still, as a little child, to come to Him. Come with your whole history and lifelong trauma, your misshapen parenting and your broken bloodline of sin and death. If you are God's child, you carry within you the death of Christ as 2 Corinthians tells us, not so you can go around stinking of death, but so you can display the life of Jesus in that same body. You are a clay jar—one that by itself is broken, belittled, beat up, weak, or fragile. But you have a treasure inside—God who indwells that weak jar and offers resurrection power. Jesus is alive. And because Jesus is alive and His Spirit is in you, He has come into your specific history, your specific family, and He has brought blessing and life.

You will still parent as it seems best to you according to God's Word (or be parented as it seems best to them), but you will do it knowing He has drawn you to Himself, given you His Spirit to guide you, offered you His Scripture to follow, and put His hands on you for blessing. He has done it because the kingdom of God belongs to such as you, regardless of your family history or genetic makeup or the circumstances that have formed you. It seemed best to God for the blood of His Son to cover every blot on your bloodline and to bless you. Rest in that as His child. Rest in His touch and blessing over you.

CHAPTER TEN

Remember, Remember

Lord, on thee do I depend
thy limbs hold me, heal me, of
all unbelieving doubts. And now
I do not break, I bend, I bend;
thou hast made of me a bough.[1]
—Madeleine L'Engle

Remember You Have a Body

The physical ailments that cause me early miscarriage and other side-effects aren't curable, but they are manageable. For me, the road to healing seems to stretch on into the long future, but there are small steps Nate and

---

[1] Madeleine L'Engle, "Thomas: After Seeing the Wounds," *A Cry Like a Bell* (Wheaton, IL: Harold Shaw Publishers, 1987), 92.

I can take to help my body feel better along the way. Our doctor recommended integrative chiropractic care, deep tissue massage, and frequent Epsom salt baths, among other things. Basically, she said: take care of yourself. Let yourself be touched in order to work toxicity out, increase blood flow to certain organs, and realign your body. Right after she told me it was likely that I had been miscarrying nearly every cycle since we began trying to get pregnant, I was silent, and she said, "Remember you're only human and, at the very least, that means you're a body. Don't forget you have a body."

And I've been trying to remember it every day since then.

When I think of my existence as a mind, body, and soul (or heart), I truly believe I'm stronger in the categories of mind and heart, as I don't like feeling the frailty of my body—its limitedness, its finiteness. I dislike not being God and sovereign over my body. I dislike not being able to heal myself, right what's wrong, or fix what's broken. I want to will my body into submission, but it will not be willed. The multiple genetic disorders I have happened not only when I was in my mother's womb, but when *she* was in her mother's womb. The doctors call it an autoimmune illness, and though we don't understand all of its complexities, we know one thing for sure: it found a weak link in my body and wreaked havoc on it. I feel powerless in fixing it. However, mitigating it, supplementing its healthy counterparts, working against it—these things I can do. But I can't change my condition. I cannot be what I am not. At least not until the other side of the resurrection.

My physical woes often make me think about the rest of the world. My illness is a tiny sliver of the pain and sickness and debilitation people all through history have experienced all over the world. There are more humans suffering today than ever before in history. Sickness, suffering, slavery, systemic racism, the list goes on and on. No one is unscathed from the physical suffering. We feel our brokenness at our core. No one escapes it. Even if we know Jesus is real and came and is coming again to bring healing and wholeness to these unraveling bodies, we still feel like "elect exiles," strangers and aliens in a world that's constantly breaking and breaking us.

Everyone loves to quote Hemingway: "The world breaks everyone and afterward many are strong at the broken places." But few continue with the rest of his thought: "Those that will not break it kills. It kills the very good and the very gentle and the very brave impartially. If you are none of these you can be sure it will kill you too but there will be no special hurry."[2] As morbid as it sounds, Hemingway is right. The world (and sin) will eventually, whether quickly or slowly, kill us all. It's living itself that brings us eventually to death. Sin entered the world and so death entered too. None of us are immune from the last breath. This is why, I think, our world is so set on getting what it can today, believing what it sees today, and doubtful of the reality of the gospel and eternity with Christ.

---

[2] Ernest Hemingway, *Farewell to Arms* (1929; repr., New York: Scribner, a division of Simon & Schuster, Inc., 2014), 317.

✳ ✳ ✳

Scripture gives us an example of someone grappling with eternal things. Because of his response to the news that Jesus had risen from the dead ("Unless I see in his hands the mark of the nails, and place my finger into the mark of the nails, and place my hand into his side, I will never believe."[3]), he's known as Doubting Thomas. I've always felt a little offended by that moniker. Thomas and I are a bit alike, both having walked with Jesus for some time, yet the moment He seems gone, we disbelieve the possibility of His presence again. In fact, we're all like Thomas. Every one of the billions of people who have ever lived throughout all of history is just like Thomas. We're a forgetting people and a doubtful people. It's why we keep returning to the things that feel certain today—namely, the things we can touch and feel and hold in our hands. The things we know for sure and can count on. It's uncomfortable to exist in uncertain spaces. It's scary. It's unknown. We're constantly grabbing sandbags to weigh the balloons of uncertainty down: mortgages, picket fences, apartment leases, roommates, 401Ks, better cars, longer vacations. Anything to remind us we're the most real thing we know because, for most of us, we *are* the most real thing we know. We, like Thomas, live in the in-between place where we can't see the actual hands and feet of Jesus in front of us. So we grab for all the other things we can see.

But the good news is that, also like Thomas, one day we will see those hands and feet. One day our eyes will take

---

[3] John 20:25.

Him in, and our hands will grasp His feet, and our bodies will become like His—resurrected and sinless and glorified.

"Remember you have a body," my doctor said.

I remember it all the time. It's a body of death for now, but soon, it will be full of life.

Remember You Are Part of a Body

It's not surprising that American culture loves to quote the Declaration of Independence: "We hold these truths to be self-evident, that all men are created equal, that they are endowed by their Creator with certain unalienable Rights, that among these are Life, Liberty, and The Pursuit of Happiness." These words are plastered all over the place—in our movies, on our tourist's paraphernalia, in our courtrooms, and at our patriotic events. Though we've perhaps done a good job trumpeting these words, truth be told, we are not a culture who has done a faithful work in actually upholding them. True equality and real happiness will never be attained outside the new heaven and new earth—but sometimes it feels like it's not even attempted in much of our culture.

Before class or racial divides, before religious or academic divisions, we are all part of the human race. We are humans and it is our unalienable right—and God-given gift—to be treated as a human *first*. To be seen, touched, and heard by people who truly care about us as humans.

A few months ago my husband arrived home from an overnight trip. He walked into the house greeted by the electrician and me. Our stove had been giving us a hard time, and eventually we chalked it up to its age. It was a twenty-year-old appliance, after all, though we had only bought the house a year before. We bought a new one and the same problem kept happening. It turned out to be an electrical problem and not a cheap fix either. So, in walks my husband to a $6,000 estimate to replace our control panel. As soon as Jacob (the electrician) left, Josh (the pool guy) arrived, who was there to help us navigate a drainage problem that also came with the house when we bought it—also not a cheap fix.

After he left, my poor husband sat on our couch and, exhausted and feeling defeated, reminded me that it was date night and he didn't have a plan. We rarely have a plan for date night and usually find a used bookstore to peruse. Other times we'll head to the library or go for a drive. We have two housemates and it's refreshing to simply get an evening to ourselves sometimes.

If you're not excited about eating at the latest restaurant or catching yet another movie or wandering around the plethora of outdoor malls in Dallas, there really isn't much to do. We've spent years individually and as a couple trying to find outdoor scenery via hikes, quiet little haunts, hole-in-the-wall diners, and a few trees on which to string our hammocks. These things can feel hard to come by, so we never feel more like we live in a concrete jungle than we do on date nights.

We looked online to see if any museums were open (because it was 105 degrees outside) or if any local music events were on the city's calendar. We were ready to fall back on our typical date night plan—dinner and a used bookstore—when I happened upon a link that could either be a total bust or a total win.

We headed out, grabbed dinner to go, and drove north. I was navigating, Nate was driving, and our drive took us to the north side of a college town nearby. We turned down a side street, past a few houses with old cars in their driveways and blue tarps over their porches and piles of junk in their yards, and there, at the end of the lane, next to an acre of multi-colored roses and against a backdrop of a peach orchard, was a sign. *Rose and Peach Farm, Self-Guided Tours.*

Jackpot.

It seemed like no one was there, but we parked the car and got out anyway. As we were walking in awe toward a grapevine-covered oak tree (that Nate said looked like it was transported from the set of *Stranger Things*), a dark-skinned, toothless man with a limp ambled over. He was the caretaker of this Edenic plot. Nate and I love a self-guided tour, but this guy seemed like a treasure trove of knowledge to us, and we wanted him to guide us instead.

The man showed us the land's irrigation methods, talked through the process of seeding and planting the towering tangle of tomatoes in front of us, explained how the roses were being bred and rebred, pointed out the piles of brush he'd gathered along with the raised beds he'd built. He was a man bursting with joy and pride at this thing he'd helped cre-ate. Though he was not the owner of it, it still somehow was his. I wouldn't have been surprised if he slept on a cot in the greenhouse at night. He was in this place somehow. He told us how sometimes he heard the ghostly whispers of "Native settlers duking it out, you know, from history." And then he laughed, throwing back his head, his toothless grin wide and his eyes bright with some private joke.

"My name is Lore," I said, and held out my hand.

"Armando," he said with a lisp. My extended hand lingered in the air and he took it with his brown hand, held it firmly, and shook it well.

In spite of every way we were different socio-economically, historically, and otherwise, as I held his hand, I felt a God-given equality of humanness with this toothless, sweaty, limping man, who had spent the past eight years of his life toiling in the Texas sun over this plot of land. I felt it more than I've felt it with the hundreds of people milling around me every day in the coffee shops and big box stores of the suburbs. His hand was rough and smooth and weathered and firm. I gripped it hard back, wanting to somehow convey my respect for him, my honor toward him, how humbled I felt to be in his presence, in that handshake. I wanted him to know I saw him as my equal, and that I desperately wanted to share all the inalienable rights that come with being white and middle class with him in that moment. I had already said thank you and given other affirmations of appreciation with my words, but I wanted to touch this man who I sensed probably didn't get touched by very many white people, driving up in their Subarus, wearing linen shirts and raw denim jeans with holes in them that weren't worn in by hard work but by money-hungry designers. I wanted to be near this man, not just to learn from him agriculturally, but to learn from him as a person. I wanted to hug him. I know it's naive and there's so much work to be done in terms of our nation's economy and opportunity to those who need it; but in that moment, I needed to remember we were just two humans standing in the middle of a rose garden, our hands gripping with respect. I couldn't change anything about our two different realities in that moment—the work is much harder, much deeper, and much more profound than a mere handshake—but I could touch this man. I could shake his hand and look him in the eye. I could start there, at the very least.

When Nate and I left this magical place an hour later, it wasn't the roses and tomatoes I kept thinking most about; it was Armando. Mary Oliver's words from her poem, "When Death Comes," ran through my mind: "and each body a lion of courage, and something / precious to the earth."[4] This man, this caretaker, with courage enough to look at a dirt plot of land in north Texas and make it something beautiful was precious to the earth.

It wasn't lost on me that others arrived at the farm after we did and they barely acknowledged Armando's existence. I wondered if that was the norm and part of his delight in speaking with us was that we were speaking with him at all. How many people, I wondered, come through this place, picking roses and tomatoes and peaches, and never think of this man as anything more than the one who takes their money when they leave? Does he have a name to them? Do they care?

Do I care? I may have shook the hand of this man, but do I *really* care beyond that? Do I think a sweet and meaningful

---

[4] Mary Oliver, "When Death Comes," *New and Selected Poems, volume 1* (Boston: Beacon Press, 1992), 10.

moment of touch—genuine as it was—will change everything that needs to be changed in the way this man is treated
on a larger level? The questions mulled in my mind. I don't
have answers to them all, but I know that dignifying another human with touch is a good place to start. Before we
can begin to fix global problems, we have to begin with the
most local solutions, we have to begin with our neighbor, our
fellow human, the ones we can touch with our own hands.

※ ※ ※

In Wendell Berry's stunning essay "Health Is
Membership," from his book, *The Art of the Commonplace*, he
closes with this story:

> During [my brother's] stay in the hospital
> there were many moments in which doctors
> and nurses—especially nurses!—allowed or
> caused the professional relationship to become
> a meeting between two human beings, and
> these moments were invariably moving.
>
> The most moving, to me, happened in the
> waiting room during John's surgery. From
> time to time a nurse from the operating
> room would come in to tell Carol what was
> happening. Carol, from politeness or bravery
> or both, always stood to receive the news,
> which always left us somewhat encouraged
> and somewhat doubtful. Carol's difficulty
> was that she had to suffer the ordeal not only

as a wife but as one who had been a trained nurse. She knew, from her own education and experience, in how limited a sense open-heart surgery could be said to be normal or routine.

Finally, toward the end of our wait, two nurses came in. The operation, they said, had been a success. They explained again what had been done. And then they said that after the completion of the bypasses, the surgeon had found it necessary to insert a "balloon pump" into the aorta to assist the heart. This possibility had never been mentioned, nobody was prepared for it, and Carol was sorely disappointed and upset. The two young women attempted to reassure her, mainly by repeating things they had already said. And then there was a long moment when they just looked at her. It was such a look as parents sometimes give to a sick or suffering child, when they themselves have begun to need the comfort they are trying to give.

And then one of the nurses said, "Do you need a hug?"

"Yes," Carol said.

And the nurse gave her a hug.

Which brings us to a starting place.[5]

---

[5] Wendell Berry, "Health Is Membership," *The Art of the Commonplace* (Berkley, CA: Counterpoint, 2002), 256–57.

The "starting place" Berry writes of is a return to health by way of the membership of community. He argues that we have to remember we are more than our bodies, but we are also not less than them. He says if we can really, truly know and understand this, then we will become a more holistic society as a whole. If we forget we are embodied creatures, it is far easier to talk of things in compartmentalized or removed ways. But when we remember that every person, regardless of race, color, religion, sexuality, health, and what-ever other categories we find, *matters*, all our work is better for it. A lyric from the singing duo, Johnnyswim, says, "If it matters, let it matter."[6] Everything God has created, from dust, bone, and breath, is matter and therefore *matters*.

Our culture is so busy and chaotic and full that we barely stop to acknowledge people, let alone touch them in any way. We forget that because we are matter and we matter, oth-ers matter too. Cashiers, doctor's office administrators, mail carriers, neighbors, executives, fellow shoppers in the aisles of the grocery store, house-cleaners, CEOs, and lawn care-takers. Jacob, the electrician. Josh, the pool guy. Armando who works the land to cultivate roses and the guy who owns the land they're planted on. Every one of these people, these humans, is equal and yet in the neglect of our looking, see-ing, and sometimes touching (a mere handshake, a hand on the shoulder, a brush of the hand), we de-equalize them. We tier them. Culture tells us we must. It tells us there are class divides and social divides or levels of what's appropriate or

---

[6] Johnnyswim, "Let It Matter," *Georgica Pond*, Capitol Music Group Sweden, 2016.

necessary or professional. It lies to us and says all touch with persons with whom we have no relationship is wrong.

Withholding touch from other humans is a form of protecting ourselves from truly practicing what we preach: that all men are created equal, endowed by God with certain unalienable rights. Sometimes exercising our rights means we do not want to be touched, but sometimes, our right *is to be* touched, to be humanized by those who dehumanize, to close the gap that exists when we make things only theoretical and not real. It is impossible to remain an enemy when we are shoulder to shoulder in the foxhole.

Kathleen Norris writes, "Who is my neighbor? This may be the most important question we can ask, a matter of life or death for us, and our planet. That great image of Gerard Manley Hopkins: 'The Holy Ghost over the bent / World broods with warm breast and with ah! bright wings' only works for me when I consider it as including all the world—as in an astronaut's view of it—and not just my small portion."[7]

Who is my neighbor? Everyone.

God made us with bodies and came in a body and died in a body and rose again in a body, and one day all His people will dwell with Him forever—every one of us in our own glorified body. Each of those realities matter to the entire gospel narrative and so they should each inform the way we interact with the world around us, our fellow humans on earth. It should inform how we touch and are touched, even by those with whom we have *seemingly* no personal relationship. We

---

[7] Kathleen Norris, *Amazing Grace* (New York: Riverhead Books, 1998), 358.

are persons and therefore all our relationships *are* personal. Armando, Josh the pool guy, Jacob the electrician, the nurses at the hospital where your child receives care, the integrative chiropractor I visit monthly, my best friend who is a massage therapist, your kid, your kid's friends, the immigrant woman who stocks shelves at my local grocery market (which is her second job because her husband—who was the primary breadwinner and the reason they moved to the United States—has cancer), your spouse or parent or siblings, the politician you hate, the pastor you love, the frenemy at work you aren't quite sure about—every one of these people is made in the image of God and they matter, body and soul. Every person who has ever lived—from every rung of society and corner of the earth—is ultimately made of the same stuff, and therefore part of a larger body called humanity, doubters and seers alike.

We cannot unsee any of these people all around us. And once we see them, something happens. As John O'Donohue would say, "the act of seeing begins [our] work of mourning."[8] When we finally see someone we should have noticed all along, aren't we a little shocked, or saddened that we've never seen them before? When we pass over the Armandos of the world, and then come to realize we've never acknowledged their existence, our souls tend to drop their proverbial heads. That's what seeing a person, truly seeing them, does to a person who hasn't noticed the sacredness of another's humanity before. Our act of mourning should first include how we have

---

[8] John O'Donohue, *To Bless the Space Between Us* (New York: Doubleday, 1998), 168.

overlooked, mastered, ignored, marginalized, and more, and then include repentance—turning the other way, changing how we treat people, which includes touch. In fact, we enact our seeing by touching.

When Thomas hears from his fellow disciples that they have "seen the Lord," his response is unsurprising and common: "Unless I see in his hands the mark of the nails, and place my finger into the mark of the nails, and place my hand into his side, I will never believe." Only those on the other side of this narrative would arrogantly ascribe the name "Doubting" to Thomas—most of us would have said the same thing. If we were in Thomas's shoes, we would have seen the body of Christ crucified and buried. We would have likely assumed that there's no way that body could have been alive, let alone touchable. Yes, Thomas doubted. But it was reasonable doubt.

The response of Jesus to this reasonable doubt is astounding. Where the other disciples believed Jesus was real by merely seeing Him and His wounds, Thomas wants more. He wants to put his fingers right through the nail marks. He wants to thrust his hand into Jesus' side where the spear wounded Him. It is not the form of Christ's body that matters most to Thomas; he wants the messiness of it, the scars, the proof of living *and* dying. And Jesus offers it to him. "Put your finger here, and see my hands. Put your hand and place it in my side. Don't disbelieve, but believe."

Just a few chapters earlier, in John 14, Jesus said to His disciples, "Believe me that I am in the Father and the Father is in me. Otherwise, believe because of the works themselves."[9] Another translation reads, "Believe in the evidence of the miraculous works I have done" (NLT). Here is what He offers to Thomas: the evidence of the miracle. Jesus knew His body wasn't staying on the earth for long, but He came to the doubter and offered it up for what He needed from it. Barry Jones says, "Spirituality in the way of Jesus is about learning to be used as an instrument of his healing grace in the lives of others as we make our wounds available to them."[10] Jesus made His wounds available to Thomas, proof not only of His resurrection, but of the lengths to which He'd gone to show Thomas the love He had for him. Thus, Thomas's eyes were open to the Risen Lord—he could finally "see" Him— through touching Him.

We cannot offer that same hope—the physical broken body of Jesus—to a doubting, fractured, marginalized world. We cannot hand over Jesus' body to someone who is struggling with unbelief regarding the resurrection. We cannot open people's eyes by literally handing them Jesus in the flesh. Jesus has gone to His Father, just as He said He would, and thus His body is not right here in front of us. It is sitting at the right hand of the Father for now, until the consummation. But Jesus has left us here, embodied, carrying with us the death of Christ,[11] bearing on our bodies the marks

---

[9] John 14:11.

[10] Dr. Barry Jones, *Dwell* (Downers Grove, IL: InterVarsity Press, 2014), 98.

[11] 2 Corinthians 4:10.

of Christ,[12] with eternity written on our hearts,[13] and being read as a letter from Christ as a recommendation to all of His life, death, and resurrection.[14] For those who cannot read, we teach them. How? By using our lives and our bodies to engage in the messiness of what Christ's death, burial, and resurrection means. Though the world cannot touch Jesus, it can touch us. And Christ is in us. In a profound way, when the world comes into contact with us, it comes in contact with Him. In other words, *we* are the way the Thomases of this world gain their sight.

You might ask how? How can we be the side of Christ that a struggling Thomas touches? How can we help open the eyes of those around us who doubt? We use touch in the ways Jesus told us to. We reenact the gospel. We rest our hand on the shoulder of the weary grocery store worker. We lay a hand on the head of a neighbor's child. We do not leave a seat between us and another at an event. We initiate hugs and do not get offended when they aren't returned. We reach out our hands to shake another's and grip it not too limply (communicating we find them repulsive) or too strongly (communicating power over them), but firm and soft simultaneously (and this takes practice, but it's a practice worth doing). We pass the peace to one another at church. We give and receive communion from the hands of another. We dip believers below the baptismal waters and lift them up with our hands saying, "Raised to walk in the newness of life." We

---

[12] Galatians 6:17.
[13] Ecclesiastes 3:11.
[14] 2 Corinthians 3:1–3.

transfer the hands of a bride from her father to her groom in marriage. With our hands we offer hope, healing, and a way forward. We cannot offer a clean, orderly, untouchable hope; we have to offer it all—everything Jesus offers to Thomas in that moment. We have to be willing to engage those with no hope by bringing the hope we carry within us, within our bodies, to them. And what is the hope we carry within us? Jesus promised it to His disciples in John 15: His Holy Spirit.

Remember Your Future Body

There's one more person in John 20 whose exchange with Jesus we can't miss. Where there is a doubter in this chapter, there is also a believer. Only a few verses before Jesus offers the messiest parts of His body to be touched by Thomas, He tells Mary, the first to see Him risen, "Don't cling to me . . . since I have not yet ascended to the Father. But go to my brothers and tell them that I am ascending to my Father and your Father, to my God and your God."[15] To Mary, the worshipper, the one who sees and believes, He assures that His body isn't staying put for long. He's going to His Father—which Mary would know and believe would commence the coming of His Spirit to dwell within them, helping, comforting, and "teach[ing them] all things."[16] To the doubter He offers His body as proof. To the believer, He offers His Spirit as guarantee.[17]

---

[15] John 20:17.
[16] John 14:26.
[17] Ephesians 1:14.

One of the best lines from one of my favorite Rich Mullins' songs "Land of My Sojourn" goes, "Nobody tells you when you get born here / How much you'll come to love it /And how you'll never belong here."[18] We will always feel like sojourners in this world, our bodies aching to be face-to-face with Christ, and our hearts restless until we are there. As long as we live on earth, we will have both doubts and answers, depending on the season and circumstance. We will have moments of fear and moments of worship. We will sometimes suffer and we will sometimes celebrate. We will waver in conviction and stand firm on it too. We will question our actions or we will question the actions of others. I've said in this book in multiple ways, threaded through it all, that we cannot conform the way we touch ourselves, others, and the world to a series of rules and regulations or to a list of dos and don'ts. But, if we are a child of God, a worshipper of the risen Lord, the Spirit of God dwells within us. The Spirit compels us, convicts us, comforts us, and gives us clarity.

Every day of life on this earth, in this land of our sojourn, we will be dependent on the Spirit of God who dwells inside our bodies, who is wrapped intrinsically around our messiness, our scars, the imprints of what the world and sin have wreaked on us. The Spirit of God working in tandem with the Word of God is our barometer and our compass. That feels dangerous to say in a world where, "Jesus told me to do it," can sound like a handy excuse for sinful or inappropriate touch. But just because our understanding and practicing of

---

[18] Rich Mullins "Land of My Sojourn," *Liturgy, Legacy, and a Ragamuffin Band*, Reunion, 1993.

the conviction, comfort, and compelling nature of the Spirit has been wrongly abused and attributed, doesn't mean we should disbelieve His power within us to repent for where we have wronged, to heal where we have broken, to hold what we have withheld and been withheld from, and to help us in the moments we don't know what to do.

"The years to come—this is a promise—" the poet, Mary Oliver wrote, "will grant you ample time / to try the difficult steps in the empire of thought / where you seek for the shining proofs you think you must have."[19] As long as we dwell here with these bodies, we have the laborious task of working out our salvation on earth, seeking the "shining proofs" of the love of God to His people on earth.

If you close this book and simply feel more equipped to engage your body with the bodies around you, I have done a decent job, perhaps, but not a job well done. But if you close this book and see the Spirit more at work within your body and within the bodies of others, and can offer your earthly body for the work of Christ in this world, knowing "What is sown is perishable; what is raised is imperishable. It is sown in dishonor; it is raised in glory. It is sown in weakness; it is raised in power. It is sown a natural body; it is raised a spiritual body,"[20] then my work has been as faithful as I could make it.

Children of God interact with the world around us *as* bodies but with the assurance that our bodies are not long

---

[19] Mary Oliver, "Terns," *New and Selected Poems,* Volume 2 (Boston: Beacon Press, 2005), 34.
[20] 1 Corinthians 15:42–44 (esv).

for this earth. We may feel the desire to cling to an incarnate Christ, as Mary did in the garden, but know with clarity that the work of Jesus on earth was completed and He dwells now with the Father, having sent the Spirit to dwell in us. And we are able to interact with the world around us, with every *body*, as Jesus did with those who doubt. We are able to offer the messiness of what Christ's death and resurrection means for the world—scars, guts, and all. We won't be afraid to enter into messy situations and we won't withhold our bodies from that which God intended them for: to bring Him glory. We may be earthen vessels, but we hold Living Water, the kind the world can't give. Because of the Holy Spirit's indwelling, when our bodies show up to the various situations of the world, they literally bring with them the Living God.

When we are in a season of doubting, like Thomas, we need other bodies *outside* ourselves to perform physical reenactments of the gospel in front of us (the Lord's Supper, baptism, etc.) so that we can remember what's true. When we are in seasons of belief, like Mary, we need a reminder that our deep belief and inner comfort comes from God *within* our bodies, the Holy Spirit, and for Him to interact with others around us, our bodies have to go to them, have to show up, have to be present. In both cases, bodies—and therefore touch—are not just helpful, but required.

As long as we live on this version of earth, we will live in this version of our bodies, hosts to the Spirit of God within us. But someday all that's perishable will pass away and these bodies that touch and are touched will be made new.

Remember Christ's Body

You have touched and been touched. You have taken touch sinfully and given it sinfully. You have been touched because of the fear, doubt, anger, or sin of another. And you have given touch in fear, doubt, anger, or sin. You have abused and been abused. You have touched your body in lust, sure you deserve to feel a certain way or are owed a certain pleasure. You have touched your body in doubt that God sees and knows and cares for you. You have touched it misbelieving, like Eve, that you are God over it. You have touched the bodies of your friends in faith and sometimes in fear, wanting what they can't give you. You have sinfully touched the bodies of those you've dated or wanted to date, or simply whose attention you wanted. You have sinfully touched your children in anger, or withheld touch from them in fear. You have reserved touch in your marriage only for sex or you have given it in order to get something in return. You have withheld touch from your brothers and sisters in Christ, worshipping the god of impressions instead of the God who protects His children. You have withdrawn from the touch of a stranger in church, in the grocery story, in the subway. Or you've touched strangers and wanted their touch just to remind you that you're real, you're matter, and you matter. You feel within you the dearth of touch, the death it's worked in you, and the determination to control how it works itself out in your life and relationships. You try to master it so it can't master you. When you can't master it, you let it master you anyway. You are some of these experiences, or maybe even all of them.

But that's not the end of the story, is it? We have a God who came in flesh as Christ, our true master, our true vine-dresser, our true brother, our true friend, our true healer, our true savior. We cannot do any good apart from Him.

The words of C. S. Lewis ring true:

> Love anything, and your heart will certainly be wrung and possibly broken. If you want to make sure of keeping it intact, you must give your heart to no one, not even to an animal. . . . The only place outside of Heaven where you can be perfectly safe from all the dangers and perturbations of love is Hell. . . . We shall draw nearer to God, not by trying to avoid the sufferings inherent in all loves, but by accepting them and offering them to Him; throwing away all defensive armour. If our hearts need to be broken, and if He chooses this as the way in which they should break, so be it.[21]

To love in this way, to touch, is to risk brokenness, making mistakes, getting it wrong. But, as I said in the beginning of this book, there's a gospel for that. We cannot live lightly on this earth, but must tend the unruly garden we've been given—others and ourselves. That is the call of a faithful Christ-follower as long as we live in the Already/Not Yet. We must live in the bodies we have and interact with the bodies

---

[21] C. S. Lewis, *The Four Loves* (New York: Harper One, 2017), 117.

others have and to remember what the broken body of Christ means for all the bodies (and souls) of history.

One of my pastors quotes the Heidelberg Catechism whenever he serves us communion:

> That Christ has commanded me and all believers, to eat of this broken bread, and to drink of this cup, in remembrance of him, adding these promises: first, that his body was offered and broken on the cross for me, and his blood shed for me, as certainly as I see with my eyes, the bread of the Lord broken for me, and the cup communicated to me; and further, that he feeds and nourishes my soul to everlasting life, with his crucified body and shed blood, as assuredly as I receive from the hands of the minister, and taste with my mouth the bread and cup of the Lord, as certain signs of the body and blood of Christ.[22]

As I let the bread settle on my tongue and let the wine pool around it, I remember: this is how sure I can be that Christ came *in a body for my body.* I remember all the sins I've committed during my week, all the ones I can remember. I feel the conviction rise up for the ways I've sinned against God and others with my words, my heart, and my body.

And I remember: *I am just this body, mind, and heart right now* and I am *not* the Christ. But I have the Christ and I have

---

[22] Heidelberg Catechism.

His Spirit within me and I have the love of the Father and, by His grace and in His goodness, these sins aren't all there is.

As I swallow, I ask for help, hope, and healing. As I literally *feel* the crumbs and the liquid wash down my throat, I *feel* felt by the God who sees and knows and loves and sent the embodied Jesus for this very reason.

Your matter matters. My matter matters. Every body matters. Everybody matters. Remember you are embodied. Remember who indwells you—that you house the Holy Spirit. Remember whose you are. Remember who loves you. Remember to whom you're going.

Go, you who have been touched by the love of God for the glory of God, touch and be touched.

A Letter to Those Who Have Been Abused

Dear friend,

Maybe you've just thumbed through this book while standing in a bookstore or scrolled through an online preview. You're wondering, *How could any of this be for me?* Maybe you feel too broken, too hurt, too wounded, too fearful to trust that it might be. Or maybe you've reached the end of this book and you're disappointed in how I've handled a particular section or words I didn't say or things you thought should be included.

Maybe you're still angry at your abuser or maybe you've forgiven them. Maybe you've just made peace with it all. I don't know. I can't possibly know. I think that's been the hardest thing about writing this book, or even thinking about writing it. There are nearly eight billion people in the world today and there have been more than one hundred billion throughout all time. Billions and billions of hearts, minds, stories, families, marriages, relationships, bodies, and beings. And I am only one. *What can I even say?*, I've thought. *What if I say it wrong?* At the end of it all, it has come down to one question for me, day after day, week after week, while I've been writing: Am I being faithful to God and His Word?

I am just one person writing one book that will no doubt land in a landfill in the not-so-distant future. Knowing that everything in this book is disappearing as quickly as dew, I want to say with Moses,

> "Let my teaching fall like rain
> and my word settle like dew,
> like gentle rain on new grass
> and showers on tender plants,"

But I also want to say with Moses,

> "For I will proclaim the LORD's name.
> Declare the greatness of our God!
> The Rock—his work is perfect
> all his ways are just.
> A faithful God, without bias,
> he is righteous and true."[1]

I *desire* that my words have been tender, but I don't have to desire that God's words are great, perfect, just, without bias, righteous, and true—I *know* they are. My words will be like dew, passing quickly away. His words are forever.

One of my dear friends has been reckoning with decades of abuse over the past few years, and her face was the face

---

[1] Deuteronomy 32:2–4.

I envisioned while writing most of these chapters. Every word you read in *Handle with Care* was written with her in my mind. And therefore, in a sense, in the best way I could with my limited scope in time and space, it was written with you in mind. This letter to you has always been included in the manuscript, from the first outline. This book would be incomplete without an acknowledgment of the hurt enacted against you by the hands of men, women, brothers, sisters, friends, pastors, coworkers, boyfriends, girlfriends, husbands, wives, children, teachers, coaches, doctors, and more. And so I wanted to say a few things to you, just to you.

First, if there's anything in this book that's not helpful for you today, that's okay. It doesn't need to meet every person exactly where he or she is today. But I pray it doesn't cause *more* harm against you. If you feel that it has, please write to me at the address below. I commit to hearing your words.

Second, if there's anything in this book that feels too good to be true about touch, that's okay too. For a long time, and even still, I have struggled with the touch of a certain type of person because I was abused by that type of person. It has informed and affected many relationships throughout my life and I have to remember again and again that first of all, God isn't surprised by my struggle there. Second, God isn't ashamed to call me His. And third, healthy touch is *still* possible, even if it's a long way off. I can believe what *is* true without *feeling* like it is true at the same time. I am praying for healing for us both there.

Third, if there's anything in this book where you felt I offered prescriptive advice that you can't heed in faith, please forgive me. It's not my job to do that and I tried to not do it, but either way, we're called to be obedient to Scripture, not trade paperbacks. Wherever I may err, though it be unintentional, please disregard my counsel and heed the Word of God and the Holy Spirit instead.

Fourth, abuse is always wrong. It doesn't matter if it was physical, verbal, mental, financial, or sexual—or whatever other kinds of perversion exist. It is always wrong, it is always sin, and it always offends God. God hates abuse. If, after someone else reads *Handle with Care*, they feel free to use their hands or body in a way that is abusive toward you, that is wrong. It doesn't mean my words were wrong, but that their interpretation of my words was wrong. *Handle with Care* isn't license to touch everyone however we want. It's a rubric for thinking about touch and, hopefully, bringing all of our touch under the submission of God.

Fifth, if you've never gone to a counselor to process your abuse, I really recommend it. The problem is, for a lot of us, going to a counselor resulted in curt Bible verses or pop psychology or sweeping our experience under the rug, so we quit. My earnest hope for you is that you will try again and again to find hope and healing for your body and soul—that you will keep seeking until you find the right counselor. Seeing professional help doesn't magically fix anything, but it is a wonderful starting point to processing your pain and getting your bearings for moving forward.

Last, and most important, you are loved. I wish I was sitting across from you right now, reading this right to you. You are loved by the Most High God. You are loved by the perfect Father. You are loved by the sacrificial Savior. You are loved by the helping and comforting Spirit. All of God is available to you as an expression of His love for you. He is more patient, kind, gentle, faithful, generous, and good than you or I could imagine. Every person in your life—good or bad—was created in His image, created to point to Him (whether or not they actually do what they were created to do is another story). Yes, they are God's image in the world. But they stop right there. They are His *image*, His *reflection*. That's the most they can ever be. God is the real thing, and He offers you the magnificence of His presence—and *He loves you*. Of all the one hundred billion people who have ever walked the face of this earth, abusing and being abused, touching and being touched, He sees you and loves you and made your body to glorify Him just as it is—broken and being made whole. You are loved.

Love,

Lo
sayabletheblog@gmail.com
Sayable.net

Questions for Reflection or Conversation

Chapter One: Using Our Hands to Live

Take some time to think through the story of your life regarding touch. Think specifically about these questions:

What's my first memory of being touched?

What were my thoughts about touching the opposite gender at a young age? The same gender?

How did the way I was touched as a teen or young child inform the way I touch others today?

Chapter Two: Speaking the Same (Love) Language

Read through the definitions of touch offered in this chapter. Pick out two or three of the definitions that triggered difficult memories in your past. Write out the memory in as much detail as you can remember. Perhaps you were sexually abused, or perhaps you have a memory of healthy platonic touch between same-gender friendships, but not between opposite-gender friendships, or perhaps you had a difficult experience at a doctor's office where the touch was painful in order to heal, which in turn has tempted you to fear any future touch (like a root canal or an invasive gynecological appointment).

How have those experiences informed how you view all future expressions of similar types of touch in your life?

What do you think God would say to you if He had been in the room with you at the time?

Is there an action step God would have you take in order to heal from this touch (report abuse, seek counseling, change doctors, forgive a person or entity, etc.)?

Chapter Three: Broken Bloodlines

Have you ever treated your body as the thing to be worshipped instead of the temple in which the Spirit dwells? How so?

How has the answer to the previous question created distance:

Between you and women in your church?

Between you and men in your church?

Between you and children in your church?

Between you and skeptics in your church?

Or between you and those stuck in legalism?

Why do you think Jesus physically touched so many of those with whom He interacted?

What are some ways you could use your physical touch in godly ways to "be served and to serve" in your local church?

Chapter Four: Touch of Self

Today, as you go through the daily motions of touching your own body—washing your face, brushing your teeth, scratching an itch, massaging a tight muscle—try to make connections with what it means that you are embodied and able to touch your body at all.

What does God want to remind you about you, your rhythms, your habits, the things you ignore or the things you obsess over?

What does God want to remind you about Him? His creativeness, His love for you, His sovereignty?

Read Psalm 139 aloud and physically touch the part of your body each line brings to mind (for example, "look up" may remind you of your eyes). Remind yourself that God made all the intricate parts of your body and they all matter to Him.

Chapter Five: The Loving Life of Singleness

Even if you're unmarried, but especially if you are married, think of some unmarried brothers and sisters in your life.

When was the last time you think they were touched in a meaningful, healthy, intentional way? Now ask them. How disparate were your answers?

Ask them how you can love them best as a brother or sister and engage them in touch.

Ask them if they prefer to be asked first before being hugged or if they just want others to assume they want hugs.

Ask them if you can sit next to them at church or a wedding or another event you're both attending.

Ask them how you can best remind them they are loved by God. Remember, every human is different and we can't take one person's preferences and apply it broadly. This will require personal intentionality toward every person.

Chapter Six: Opposites Don't Always Attract

Think of some friendships in your life where you have withheld pure-intentioned touch because you disbelieve God's love for you or where you have drawn back from pure-intentioned touch because you distrust motives or fear the outcome.

Read this passage from Psalm 16 aloud with those friendships in mind. Think about what it means that because God guides us and loves us, we cannot be shaken, our whole being can rejoice, and our bodies can rest securely. Believing this, how should it change how you interact with your friendships, both opposite gender and same?

> LORD, you are my portion
> and my cup of blessing;
> *you hold my future.*
> The boundary lines have fallen for me
> in pleasant places;
> indeed, I have a beautiful inheritance.
> I will bless the LORD who *counsels* me—
> even at night when *my thoughts trouble me.*
> I *always* let the LORD guide me.
> Because he is at my right hand,
> *I will not be shaken.*
> Therefore my heart is glad
> and *my whole being* rejoices;
> *my body also rests securely.*
> (Ps. 16:5–9, emphasis mine)

Chapter Seven: True Love Doesn't Wait to Touch

If you're in a dating relationship, ask yourself what your urges are, and be honest about the answer. If it's just that you want to have sex, it's okay to confess that. God understands and designed our physical and biological desire for intimacy and procreation. He made sex and calls it good.

Ask the Spirit to help you recognize when the temptation to incite sexual pleasure comes and to comfort you toward seeing the other as a fellow image bearer, whose life, purity, and worship is costly.

Ask the Spirit to help you navigate purity as an expression of worship of God in your relationship instead of avoidance or indulgence.

If you're not in a dating relationship, ask the Spirit to help you encourage good, godly, pure touch between couples you know. Learn to ask questions motivated toward their hearts, instead of simply their bodies. Instead of asking, "How far did you go?" or "Where's your line?," ask, "How did you reflect or image God?" or "What are you worshipping in the moments when sexual temptation feels stronger than a desire to worship God with a pure heart?" When you see godly, costly, faithful touch happening between dating couples, encourage it instead of joking about it or being jealous of it.

Chapter Eight: Subjects and Objects in Marriage

If you are married, do you view your spouse primarily as an image bearer and your brother/sister in Christ? If not, in what ways has that harmed the ways you touch them or view touch from them?

If you're not married, do you find yourself believing touch within marriage is primarily sexual? If so, why do you believe this? How might this belief contribute to a lack of health in your singleness now and in marriage if God gives it to you?

Chapter Nine: Let the Little Children Come

Go back to chapter 3, "Speaking the Same Love Language," and reread the two or three experiences you noted at the end of the chapter.

How many of them are related to how you experienced touch within your family or how touch within your family formed a present experience with touch?

Are you able to see clearly that every person in your family suffers from a bloodline issue far more deep and profound than what we see on the surface?

How does knowing our parents disciplined us and we discipline our children "as we see fit" change your perspective on how right or wrong an experience you had was or is?

Chapter Ten: Remember, Remember

I haven't given questions for reflection for chapter 10 because I'm hoping you form your own questions for reflection and change in the way you handle the world around you with care.